The Seal of God— The Sign of God's Approval

by Carol Zarska, MA in Religion

World rights reserved. This book or any portion thereof may not be copied or reproduced in any form or manner whatever, except as provided by law, without the written permission of the publisher, except by a reviewer who may quote brief passages in a review.

The author assumes full responsibility for the accuracy of all facts and quotations as cited in this book. The opinions expressed in this book are the author's personal views and interpretations, and do not necessarily reflect those of the publisher.

This book is provided with the understanding that the publisher is not engaged in giving spiritual, legal, medical, or other professional advice. If authoritative advice is needed, the reader should seek the counsel of a competent professional.

Copyright © 2016 Carol Zarska

Copyright © 2016 TEACH Services, Inc.

ISBN-13: 978-1-4796-0667-2 (Paperback)

ISBN-13: 978-1-4796-0668-9 (ePub)

ISBN-13: 978-1-4796-0669-6 (Mobi)

Library of Congress Control Number: 2016902040

All Scripture quotations, unless otherwise indicated, are taken from THE HOLY BIBLE, NEW INTERNATIONAL VERSION®, NIV® Copyright © 1973, 1978, 1984, 2011 by Biblica, Inc.® Used by permission. All rights reserved worldwide.

Scripture quotations marked KJV are taken from The King James Version.

Scripture quotations marked NKJV are taken from the New King James Version®. Copyright © 1982 by Thomas Nelson. Used by permission. All rights reserved.

Published by

Table of Contents

Introduction..5
Chapter One   The Signet Ring 8
Chapter Two   Hearing His Voice 12
Chapter Three   The Highway to Heaven 19
Chapter Four   The Way of Holiness 24
Chapter Five   Living in His Presence 28
Chapter 6   Journey to the Throne..................33
Chapter Seven   The Sword and the Spirit............38
Chapter Eight   The Urim and Thummim..............44
Chapter Nine   Cleansing Heaven's Records........50
Chapter Ten   The Judgment of the Living 55
Chapter 11   My Own Story..............................61
Chapter 12   The Abyss 65
Chapter 13   Receiving the Seal 72
Addendum   Power over Demons....................83
Bibliography 97

Introduction

This book is meant to be a sequel to my latest book, *COUNTDOWN! Seven Trumpets for Today*. Because of the many signs of the imminence of Christ's return, sincere people around the world are asking, *What must I do to be prepared to go safely through the climactic events of earth's history and meet Jesus in peace when He comes?* The apostle Peter's advice is certainly appropriate to set us off in the right direction for our study:

> But the day of the Lord will come as a thief in the night; in the which the heavens shall pass away with a great noise, and the elements shall melt with fervent heat, the earth also and the works that are therein shall be burned up. Seeing then that all these things shall be dissolved, what manner of persons ought ye to be in all holy conversation and godliness, looking for and hasting unto the coming of the day of God, wherein the heavens being on fire shall be dissolved, and the elements shall melt with fervent heat? Nevertheless we, according to his promise, look for new heavens and a new earth, wherein dwelleth righteousness. Wherefore, beloved, seeing that ye look for such things, be diligent that ye may be found of him in peace, without spot, and blameless. (2 Peter 3:10–14, KJV)

This text points us to the final generation of God's people, the 144,000 who will stand with Jesus on Mt. Zion, and are spoken of in Revelation 14:1–5:

> Then I looked, and there before me was the Lamb, standing on Mount Zion, and with him 144,000 who had his name and his Father's name written on their foreheads.... They follow the Lamb wherever he goes. They were purchased from among mankind and offered as firstfruits to God and the Lamb. No lie was found in their mouths; they are blameless.

As we enter the time of the fifth trumpet, we need to know in greater detail the meaning of the mark, or seal of God, which all *must* receive in order to be protected during the time of trouble just ahead of us. For review, let's read the words of the prophet John as he describes the fifth trumpet.

> As I watched, I heard an eagle that was flying in midair call out in a loud voice: 'Woe! Woe! Woe to the inhabitants of the earth, because of the trumpet blasts about to be sounded by the other three angels!' The fifth angel sounded his trumpet, and I saw a star that had fallen from the sky to the earth. The star was given the key to the shaft of the Abyss. When he opened the Abyss, smoke rose from it like the smoke from a gigantic furnace. The sun and sky were darkened by the smoke from the Abyss. And out of the smoke locusts came down on the earth and were given power like that of scorpions of the earth. They were told not to harm the grass of the earth or any plant or tree, *but only those people who did not have the seal of God on their foreheads.* (Rev. 8:13–9:4, emphasis added)

How important it is, then, that we have the seal of God upon our foreheads. In fact, it is a matter of life and death! How can we be sure that we will be among those who will have this seal? It will not automatically occur just because we regard ourselves to be Christians or even Seventh-day Adventists. Observe what the apostle John says concerning those who will be approved by God when Jesus comes:

> Dear friends, now we are children of God, and what we will be has not yet been made known. But we know that when Christ appears, we shall be like him, for we shall see him as he is. All who have this hope in him purifies themselves, just as he is pure. Everyone who sins breaks the law; in fact, sin is lawlessness. But you know that he appeared so that he might take away our sins. And in him is no sin.

No one who lives in him keeps on sinning. No one who continues to sin has either seen him or known him. (1 John 3:2–6)

The reception of the seal of God is a result of knowing Jesus so well that the desire to sin will become repulsive to us. It is a result of having such a close relationship with Him that we will receive His character and reflect His image. We can never produce righteousness in our own strength. All our efforts must be focused upon maintaining a constant walk with Jesus so that He can reproduce Himself in us. Our lives will then be a reflection of the testimony given by Jesus concerning the close relationship He had with His Father. Jesus said, "I do nothing on my own but speak just what the Father has taught me. The one who sent me is with me; he has not left me alone, for I always do what pleases him" (John 8:28, 29).

It is my deepest desire that as you read the pages of this book, light will shine forth to guide you to know, love, and serve Him so devotedly that you will hear the words spoken to you as they were to Jesus, "On him [or her] God the Father has placed his seal of approval" (John 6:27).

Chapter One

The Signet Ring

In ancient times, when monarchs ruled the kingdoms of humankind, receiving the seal on the king's ring, his outstretched scepter, and his smile of approval could mean the difference between life and death. In the thrilling story of Queen Esther, it is apparent that Esther's circumspect behavior, her prayers and humility, and her forthrightness in the face of danger won her the favor of King Ahasuerus so completely that he provided access for her through Mordecai to use his signet ring as she deemed necessary for the saving of her people. Obviously, he trusted her to represent him appropriately and to know him so intimately that she would do nothing to defame his name and authority.

From this story, we can learn some lessons about the nature of the relationship that should exist between Jesus, the King of kings and Lord of lords, and His bride, the Church. He, too, has a sign, or seal, upon which hangs the destiny of each person who makes up the body of Christ, especially in the last moments, as it were, of earth's history. It is interesting to note that the word, "signet," is similar in meaning to a cluster of other words, such as "sign," "signature," and "signify." Understanding these words, as listed below, opens up deeper insights of this subject, which will undergird the goals of this book.

Sign: To mark with a sign, especially with one's name; to accept as legally binding by doing this; to sign a written agreement to show ownership of something.

Signature: A person's name written by himself in signing a letter or document.

Signet: A personal seal used to show the authenticity of documents, often in addition to the signature.

Signify: To make known, communicate by some sign, to signify assent or agreement.

The whole Bible is a magnification of the purpose of God to have a faithful people who will reveal His character in their lives and be a living testimony of His law. "Bind up the testimony, seal up the law among my disciples" (Isa. 8:16, KJV).

Let's dissect this short verse to catch the deeper meaning that lies below the surface. To "bind up" refers to "the ancient Oriental custom of binding up a document and affixing a seal to it" (*The Seventh-day Adventist Bible Commentary*, vol. 4, p. 143). Such an action would indicate that the work was done, and the writings contained within the document were completely and permanently finished.

In both the Old and New Testaments, the word testimony as used here means "witness." In Greek, the word is "martyr," and means "evidence, good reputation, certified, witness" (*NIV Concordance*, p. 1569). "Among my disciples," could also be translated, "*throughout* my disciples" (*NIV Concordance*, p. 1373, emphasis added). Thus, we could conclude that God's purpose and desire is that *all* His followers be thoroughly trained and equipped to represent His character so completely that they will be a finished product of His love, who are in agreement with His law in all aspects, and sealed as safe to live with Him forever in His kingdom.

It is consistent throughout Scripture that the last generation of God's people—the ones who live to see the coming of Jesus—will be living blameless lives through the power of the Holy Spirit. They will fully represent the character of God and His Son to the world. They will be His witnesses, for they represent Him accurately in all they do and say. Their inner thoughts will be pure and in harmony with God and His thoughts about all issues. When people react negatively toward them and attempt to destroy them, they seal their own fate and are ripened for the seven last plagues and the destruction that will come upon the world. In this way, God will bring to an end the great controversy and close forever the experiment into sin.

Consider the texts below:

The remnant of Israel shall not do iniquity, nor speak lies; neither shall a deceitful tongue be found in their mouth. (Zeph. 3:13, KJV)

'In those days, at that time,' declares the LORD, 'search will be made for Israel's guilt, but there will be none, and for the sins of Judah, but none will be found, for I will forgive the remnant I spare.' (Jer. 50:20)

'The days are coming,' declares the LORD, 'when I will make a new covenant with the people of Israel and with the people of Judah.... This is the covenant I will make with the house of Israel after that time,' declares the LORD. 'I will put my law in their minds and write it on their hearts.... For I will forgive their wickedness and will remember their sins no more.' (Jer. 31:31–34)

And in this way all Israel will be saved. As it is written: 'The deliverer will come from Zion; he will turn godlessness away from Jacob. And this is my covenant with them when I take away their sins.' (Rom. 11:26, 27)

To him who is able to keep you from stumbling and to present you before his glorious presence without fault and with great joy—to the only God our Savior be glory, majesty, power and authority, through Jesus Christ our Lord. (Jude 24, 25)

But in keeping with his promise we are looking forward to a new heaven and a new earth, where righteousness dwells. So then, dear friends, since you are looking forward to this, make every effort to be found spotless, blameless and at peace with him. (2 Peter 3:13, 14)

And this is my prayer: that your love may abound more and more in knowledge and depth of insight, so that you may be able to discern what is best and may be pure and blameless for the day of Christ. (Phil. 1:9, 10)

Therefore you do not lack any spiritual gift as you eagerly wait for our Lord Jesus Christ to be revealed. He will also keep you firm to the end, so that you will be blameless on the day of our Lord Jesus Christ. (1 Cor. 1:7, 8)

May he [the Lord] strengthen your hearts so that you will be blameless and holy in the presence of our God and Father when our Lord Jesus comes with all his holy ones. (1 Thess. 3:13)

May God himself ... sanctify you through and through. May your whole spirit, soul and body be kept blameless at the coming of our Lord Jesus Christ. The one who calls you is faithful, and he will do it. (1 Thess. 5:23, 24)

Then I looked, and there before me was the Lamb, standing on Mt. Zion, and with him 144,000 who had his name and his Father's name written on their foreheads.... They were purchased from among mankind and offered as firstfruits to God and the Lamb. No lie was found in their mouths; they are blameless. (Rev. 14:1, 4, 5)

And so, at last, in the final remnant of time, God's character will be reproduced in His people. It seems significant that although all of God's people down through the ages have been admonished to be perfect and blameless as they looked forward to the second coming of Christ, it is only the 144,000 who are called the "firstfruits" of the earth. These have gone through the final cleansing provided by Jesus in His second apartment work in the heavenly sanctuary and have received the seal of God and the latter rain of the Holy Spirit, which are necessary to live through the time of trouble. Because of this special work of Jesus, they are prepared to do what no other generation has ever been called to do: they must live through the comparatively short space of time when there is no heavenly mediator atoning for sins committed. Therefore, they must be able to live blamelessly before God through the Holy Spirit, who has fully filled, prepared, and sealed them for eternity.

It is the purpose of this book to understand how to cooperate with Jesus in His work of revealing and cleansing His people from the things in our hearts that keep us from receiving the seal of God—the sign of God's approval. To be freed from selfishness and completely empowered by God's love and grace is our goal!

Chapter Two

Hearing His Voice

Over the years in my work of counseling, I have often heard people say, "I don't hear the voice of God," or "God doesn't talk to me." I have had the joy of helping these precious souls learn to hear God's voice in the multiple ways He communicates with humankind. And I encourage every reader of this book not to rest satisfied until you, too, can have an ear sensitive to the still, small voice of the Holy Spirit, for it is necessary for our spiritual growth in having a close walk with God. In fact, this is the very purpose of our creation! Our brains are formed after the pattern of the mind of God so that we may communicate with Him and, therefore, know Him intimately.

> *The value of man is estimated in heaven according to the capacity of the heart to know God.* This knowledge is the spring from which flows all power. God created man that every faculty might be the faculty of the divine mind; and He is ever seeking to bring the human mind into association with the divine. He offers us the privilege of co-operation with Christ in revealing His grace to the world, that we may receive increased knowledge of heavenly things. Looking unto Jesus

... we enlarge our capacity for knowing God. More and more we enter into fellowship with the heavenly world, and we have continually increasing power to receive the riches of the knowledge and wisdom of eternity. (Christ's *Object Lessons*, pp. 354, 355, emphasis added)

The very limited and earthly apprehension which the disciples had of the teachings of Christ made it difficult for the Great Teacher to lead their minds into an understanding of heavenly things, and determined the measure of divine communications. (*Our High Calling*, p. 211)

I am quite sure that no sincere Christian would want to limit the measure of divine communications that God would like to give them to help in their everyday lives. The danger is that if we aren't having this connection with God, we may not even know that it is possible. However, the Scriptures are clear that we must have a personal relationship with God in order to distinguish the voice of the Good Shepherd from the voice of the enemy of our souls. Jesus tells us, "My sheep listen to my voice; I know them, and they follow me. I give them eternal life, and they shall never perish; no one will snatch them out of my hand" (John 10:27, 28). Earlier in the chapter, He had pointed out that knowing His voice was imperative to their safety: "His sheep follow him because they know his voice. But they will never follow a stranger; in fact, they will run away from him because they do not recognize a stranger's voice" (John 10: 4, 5). Notice the points Jesus makes here about how hearing His voice is a vital component in the life of every Christian:

#1. His sheep follow Him because they listen to His voice.

#2. Because they know His voice and follow Him, He gives them eternal life.

#3. Because they listen to His voice, no one can snatch them out of His hand.

#4. Because they know His voice, they will never follow a stranger but will run away from him.

#5. Because they know His voice, they do not even recognize a stranger's voice.

Of course, we know that Satan is the stranger who Jesus is alluding to here. Since hearing the voice of Jesus is the crucial turning point in whether we follow Jesus or succumb to the wiles of the devil, no one who is serious about his or her salvation can avoid the question, "Do I hear the voice of God clearly enough to avoid being deceived by the voice of the tempter?"

Have you ever wondered why there were four hundred years of silence between the book of Malachi and the book of Matthew? Here is the amazing answer:

> When Christ came into the world, darkness covered the earth and gross darkness the people. The living oracles of God were fast becoming a dead letter. The still, small voice of God was heard only at times by the most devout worshipper; for it had become overpowered and silenced by the dogmas, maxims, and traditions of men. (*The Seventh-day Adventist Bible Commentary*, vol. 4, p. 1153)

Now we can see why so very few recognized the Savior when He came. Very few had open minds to hear the communications of the Holy Spirit. This made Jesus' work so much more difficult, and it eventually led to His death. This fact underscores the need in our generation, when His second coming is so very near, for a remnant of His people who will make the effort necessary to reach the highest measure of closeness with Jesus that it is possible for them to attain!

> It is only by personal union with Christ, by communion with Him daily, hourly, that we can bear the fruits of the Holy Spirit.... Our growth in grace, our joy, our usefulness, all depend on our union with Christ and the degree of faith we exercise in Him. (*Sons and Daughters of God*, p. 290)

> We can never attain perfection of character if we do not hear the voice of God and obey His counsel. (Ibid., p. 90)

> The life of the soul depends upon habitual communion with God. (*Our High Calling*, p. 130)

> The soul that loves God, loves to draw strength from Him by constant communication with Him. When it becomes the habit of the soul to converse with God, the power of the evil one is broken; for Satan cannot abide near the soul that draws nigh to God. (Ibid., p. 96)

> Those who are the most closely connected with God are the ones who know His voice when He speaks to them. Those who are spiritual discern spiritual things. Such will feel grateful that the Lord has pointed out their errors. (*Testimonies for the Church*, vol. 5, p. 134)

Every sinful gratification tends to benumb the faculties and deaden the mental and spiritual perceptions, and the Word or the Spirit of God can make but a feeble impression upon the heart. (*The Great Controversy*, p. 474)

What a wonderful privilege we have of communing with the infinite God of heaven! We can do nothing on our own to overcome sin or change our ways. It is only communion with God that brings us into harmony with His mind and heart, and thus enables us to receive His cleansing, healing power. Notice this truth as it is revealed in Isaiah 30:19–22:

People of Zion, who live in Jerusalem, you will weep no more. How gracious he will be when you cry for help! As soon as he hears, he will answer you. Although the Lord gives you the bread of adversity and the water of affliction, your teachers will be hidden no more; with your own eyes you will see them. Whether you turn to the right or to the left, your ears will hear a voice behind you, saying, 'This is the way; walk in it.' Then you will desecrate your idols overlaid with silver and your images covered with gold; you will throw them away like a menstrual cloth and say to them, 'Away with you!'

According to this text, God speaks to us to help us understand the purpose for our trials and to learn the lessons they teach us. This helps to give us victory over the temptations that so easily best us.

Some Christians feel that God speaks only through the Scriptures and are very suspect of the idea that God communicates to us through impressions. While it is true that impressions can come from many sources, including evil spirits, to rule out impressions completely would be to cut off one of the vital ways God speaks to us through His Holy Spirit. However, it is absolutely imperative that all impressions must be in complete harmony with, and subject to, the truths of Scripture. Here are some quotations from Ellen White that may help to clarify our questions about this subject:

There are three ways in which the Lord reveals His will to us, to guide us, and to fit us to guide others. How may we know His voice from that of a stranger? How shall we distinguish it from the voice of a false shepherd? God reveals His will to us in His word, the Holy Scriptures. His voice is also revealed in His providential workings; and it will be recognized if we do not separate our souls from Him by walking in our own ways, doing according to our own wills, and following the promptings of an unsanctified heart, until the senses have become so confused that eternal things are not discerned, and the voice of Satan is so disguised that it is accepted as the voice of God. Another way in which God's voice is heard is through the appeals of His Holy Spirit, making impressions upon the heart, which will be wrought out in the character.... You, my brother, will find difficulty here because you have not yet learned by experience to know the voice of the Good Shepherd, and this places you in doubt and peril. You ought to be able to distinguish His voice. (*Testimonies for the Church*, vol. 5, p. 512)

Keep the conscience tender, that you may hear the faintest whisper of the voice that spake as never man spake. (*My Life Today*, p. 322)

The Holy Spirit is beside every true searcher of God's word, enabling him to discover the hidden gems of truth. Divine illumination comes to his mind, stamping the truth upon him with a new, fresh importance. He is filled with a joy never before felt. The peace of God rests upon him. The preciousness of truth is realized as never before. A heavenly light shines upon the Word, making it appear as though every letter were tinged with gold. God Himself speaks to the heart, making His Word spirit and life. (*Reflecting Christ*, p. 128)

"The union with Christ, once formed, must be maintained.... This is no casual touch, no off-and-on connection.... No more, said Jesus, can you live apart from Me. The life you have received from Me can be preserved only by continual communication. Without Me you cannot overcome one sin, or resist one temptation.... The channel of communication must be open continually between man and his God. (*The Desire of Ages*, p. 676)

The Lord has determined that every soul who obeys His word shall have His joy, His peace, His continual keeping power. Such men and women are brought near Him always.... He has prepared for them an abiding place with Himself.... By this unbroken communion with Him, they are made colaborers with Him. (*My Life Today*, p. 51)

What an incredible privilege to have unbroken communion with our precious Savior! What safety and peace there is in having His guidance and correction and knowing that He is ever near and willing to teach and advise us, answer our questions, open up new avenues of thought, explain the truth to us, and be our constant Friend. When we have this kind of relationship with Jesus, He says to us as He said to His disciples:

> I no longer call you servants, because a servant does not know his master's business. Instead, I have called you friends, for everything that I learned from my Father I have made known to you. (John 15:15)

> But when he, the Spirit of truth, comes, he will guide you into all truth ... and he will tell you what is yet to come. He will glorify me because it is from me that he will receive what he will make known to you. (John 16:12–14)

Jesus longs to have followers who will have such a close connection with Him that He can guide them at all times. How much sorrow we would escape and how many mistakes we could avoid if we consulted with Jesus before making our daily decisions! How many times do we look back on our lives and wish we had gone in a different direction in some important matter? But with Jesus at our side, He can even now make up for those deficiencies and mistakes—we only need to hear His voice. We must become dependent upon His counsel, day by day, moment by moment. He will never force us to follow His will, but as we learn to immerse ourselves in His Word and become familiar with the still, small voice of His Spirit speaking to our hearts, we will come to the place where we have continual peace and joy in His presence and a calm assurance of eternal life.

Below is a suggestion that I have found to be a great blessing in my life. I follow this practice daily and talk to Jesus about all the actions and thoughts I have during the day. I try to always ask for His advice, correction, and counsel. This experience has become a joyous time of communion with my wonderful Savior, and I highly recommend it to all who read this book:

> Many see and feel their lack, yet they seem to be ignorant of the influence they exert. They are conscious of the actions as they perform them, but suffer them to pass from their memory, and therefore do not reform. If ministers would make the actions of each day a subject of careful thought and deliberate review, with the object to become acquainted with their own habits of life, they would better know themselves. By a close scrutiny of their daily life under all circumstances they would know their own motives, the principles which actuate them. *This daily review of our acts, to see whether conscience approves or condemns, is necessary for all who wish to arrive at the perfection of Christian character.* (*Testimonies for the Church*, vol. 2, pp. 511, 512, emphasis added)

The rewards of this experience are of inestimable value, as we can see in this quotation:

> We can receive of heaven's light only as we are willing to be emptied of self. We cannot discern the character of God or accept Christ by faith, unless we consent to the bringing into captivity of every thought to the obedience of Christ. To all who do this the Holy Spirit is given without measure. (*The Desire of Ages*, p. 181)

As we constantly look to Jesus for His guidance, we will unconsciously become more and more like Him. Then Jesus will be able to trust us with these precious promises:

> If you remain in me and my words remain in you, ask whatever you wish, and it will be done for you. (John 15:7)

> As the will of man co-operates with the will of God, it becomes omnipotent. Whatever is to be done at His command may be accomplished in His strength. All His biddings are enablings. (*Christ's Object Lessons*, p. 333)

> When we know God as it is our privilege to know Him, our life will be a life of continual obedience. Through an appreciation of the character of Christ, through communion with God, sin will become hateful to us. (*The Desire of Ages*, p. 668)

Friend, do you long for an experience like this with Jesus? You can have it if you learn to know and obey His voice through the designated ways He has provided. Heaven can begin now with Jesus in your heart. In the next chapter, we will be carefully considering the subject of the earthly sanctuary as a pattern for understanding the way to have a deeper relationship with God.

Chapter Three

The Highway to Heaven

When Adam and Eve sinned, they were denied further access to Eden, their beautiful garden home. Sinners could not enter there, for they would eat the fruit of the tree of life and perpetuate sin forever, but they were allowed to come to the gate of the garden, build an altar there, and sacrifice the lambs that were required to remind them that someday the Savior would come. In this way, atonement would be made, and a way would be opened whereby sin would be eradicated, and the gates of Eden would again be opened for all who would be willing to walk the pathway of purity and reconciliation with God. In Isaiah 35:8–10, we find reference to the way back to our heavenly home:

> And a highway will be there; it will be called the Way of Holiness; it will be for those who walk on that Way. The unclean will not journey on it; wicked fools will not go about on it. No lion will be there, nor will any ravenous beast; they will not be found there. But only the redeemed will walk there, and those the LORD has rescued will return. They will enter Zion with singing; everlasting joy will crown

their heads. Gladness and joy will overtake them, and sorrow and sighing will flee away.

Wouldn't it be wonderful to find this "Way of Holiness" where there is no fear, no depression, no wicked people and no demonic harassment? There would only be peace and joy and singing. Of course, we think immediately of heaven and the New Jerusalem, yet we can also have such a close walk with Jesus here on earth that our hearts will constantly be in tune with heaven. This is especially necessary for God's final remnant people, for they will be preparing to go from earth to heaven without seeing death. Their characters must be ready through constant communion and connection with Him. Fortunately, God has promised to make this necessary experience as simple as possible for us; no one needs to despair of reaching that level of relationship with God.

In the following texts, which refer specifically to the Euphrates River, the Lord promises something special for the remnant of His people. He will make the way to the promised land easy by breaking it up into seven streams. He wants to make it so simple that none need to lose their way and be lost.

> He will break it up into seven streams so that anyone can cross over in sandals. There will be a highway for the remnant of his people ... as there was for Israel when they came up from Egypt. (Isa. 11:15, 16)

> The Euphrates is first mentioned in the Old Testament in reference to one of the rivers of the Garden of Eden ... and is designated as the northern boundary of the promised land. (*The Seventh-day Adventist Bible Commentary*, vol. 8, p. 328)

Notice this similar promise in Isaiah 62:10–12:

> Pass through, pass through the gates! Prepare the way for the people. Build up, build up the highway! Remove the stones. Raise a banner for the nations. The LORD has made proclamation to the ends of the earth: "Say to Daughter Zion, 'See, your Savior comes! See, his reward is with him, and his recompense accompanies him.'" They will be called the Holy People, the Redeemed of the LORD; and you will be called Sought After, the City No Longer Deserted.

A work of restoration is here described. Just as John the Baptist prepared the way for Christ's first coming, so the servants of God must prepare the way for His second coming. Without this preparation, many people will be lost who could have been saved. But in order for us to be able to help others, we must know the way ourselves. We must have traveled the path of holiness and found healing in our own lives. God needs men and women who are dedicated to know Him so fully that they will be able to remove the stones of confusion and error from the lives of other people who are also desiring to walk the pathway to the kingdom of heaven.

> I have posted watchmen on your walls, Jerusalem; they will never be silent day or night. You who call on the LORD, give yourselves no rest, and give him no rest till he establishes Jerusalem and makes her the praise of the earth. The LORD has sworn by his right hand and by his mighty arm: 'Never again will I give your grain as food for your enemies, and never again will foreigners drink the new wine for which you have toiled; but those who harvest it will eat it and praise the LORD, and those who gather the grapes will drink it in the courts of my sanctuary.' (Isa. 62:6–9)

> Thy way, O God, is in the sanctuary. (Ps. 77:13, KJV)

There are many people in this world today who have lost their way, and are wandering in the desert of sin. Satan has captured them through some temptation or trial. The lure of worldly pleasures, ease, and prosperity cause many to get off the path that leads to eternal life. But as long as Jesus remains in the heavenly sanctuary, there is hope for a changed life. Jesus beckons every soul to find rest, peace, and forgiveness in a relationship with Him that will last throughout eternity. Truly, God's highway to heaven is in the sanctuary. So, let's begin our journey.

There are seven steps in the sanctuary, as one might expect, since seven is the number that symbolizes God's perfection. The number seven is used many times throughout the Bible, especially concerning anything that has to do with the sanctuary. There are seven spirits of God mentioned in Revelation 4:5, and Revelation 5:6. Perhaps this is the basis for the number seven representing the complete, perfect character of God. Anything less than this is imperfection. It is interesting to note that the number of the beast of is 666. It is also humanity's number. Obviously, something very important is missing! "This calls for wisdom. Let the person who has insight calculate the number of the beast, for it is the number of man. That number is 666" (Rev. 13:18).

What could be the missing element in the number of the beast and also of humanity in its fallen state? Let's compare the list of spiritual elements possessed by Jesus as listed in Isaiah 11:1–4:

> A shoot will come up from the stump of Jesse; from his roots a Branch will bear fruit. The Spirit of the LORD will rest on him—the

Spirit of wisdom and of understanding, the Spirit of counsel and of might, the Spirit of the knowledge and fear of the LORD—and he will delight in the fear of the LORD.... With righteousness he will judge the needy, with justice he will give decisions for the poor of the earth.

In Isaiah 4:4, the power to cleanse God's church is called a spirit of judgment and a spirit of fire: "The Lord will wash away the filth of the women of Zion; he will cleanse the bloodstains from Jerusalem by a spirit of judgment and a spirit of fire."

In Proverbs 8, a similar list is recorded: "I, *wisdom*, dwell together with prudence; I possess *knowledge* and discretion. To *fear the LORD* is to hate evil; I hate pride and arrogance, evil behavior and perverse speech. *Counsel* and sound *judgment* are mine; I have *insight*, I have *power*" (Prov. 8:12–14, emphases added).

So if we make a list of seven qualities, they would be:

1. Wisdom

2. Understanding

3. Counsel

4. Power

5. Knowledge

6. Fear of the Lord, which is hatred of evil

7. Judgment

According to Proverbs 8:12–14, wisdom is the principal quality, under which all others fall into place. This is underscored in Proverbs 9:1: "Wisdom has built her house; she has set up its seven pillars."

Now, let's go back to Revelation 13:18 and find out which of the seven pillars of wisdom is missing from the beast and from fallen humanity. Since the beast is a representative of Satan (Rev. 13:2), the missing characteristic must originate in Satan himself. This is made more clear in Ezekiel 28:12–19:

> This is what the Sovereign LORD says: 'You were the seal of perfection, *full of wisdom and perfect in beauty*.... You were blameless in your ways from the day you were created till wickedness was found in you.... Your heart became proud on account of your beauty, and *you corrupted your wisdom because of your splendor*.... By your many

sins and dishonest trade you have desecrated your sanctuaries. So I made a fire come out from you, and it consumed you, and I reduced you to ashes on the ground in the sight of all who were watching.' (emphases added)

Satan still has a measure of wisdom, understanding, counsel, power, knowledge, and judgment, but all are now corrupted by his diabolical, evil mind. However, there is one thing he is totally devoid of: fear of the Lord, which is hatred of evil. Humanity in its fallen state, without the transforming power of the indwelling of the Holy Spirit, has the same mind as does the devil, for the carnal mind is naturally at enmity with God.

> The mind governed by the flesh is death, but the mind controlled by the Spirit is life and peace. The mind governed by flesh is hostile to God; it does not submit to God's law, nor can it do so. Those who are in the realm of the flesh cannot please God. You, however, are not in the realm of the flesh but are in the realm of the Spirit, if indeed the Spirit of God lives in you. (Rom. 8:6–9)

The question, then, becomes: have we given our hearts to Jesus and are we living by His Spirit? God has made it easy to understand the seven simple steps of the sanctuary. In the following chapter, we will consider the pathway of holiness, which will prepare the remnant to be ready for Jesus' soon return to take us home.

Chapter Four

The Way of Holiness

The first question we need to address in order to build a foundation for the rest of the chapter is this: what is holiness? The best and most practical answer to this is found in the writings of Ellen White: "Holiness is agreement with God" (*Testimonies for the Church*, vol. 5, p. 743). This short statement has infinite meaning. How can fallen humankind ever be in agreement with God when our very natures are at enmity with Him?

> The mind governed by flesh is hostile to God; it does not submit to God's law, nor can it do so. Those who are in the realm of the flesh cannot please God. (Rom. 8:8)

> I know that good itself does not dwell in me, that is, in my sinful nature. For I have the desire to do what is good, but I cannot carry it out. For I do not do the good I want to do, but the evil I do not want to do—this I keep on doing.... For in my inner being I delight in God's law; but I see another law at work in me, waging war against the law of my mind and making me a prisoner of the law of sin at work within me. What a wretched man I am! Who will rescue me

from this body that is subject to death? Thanks be to God, who delivers me through Jesus Christ our Lord! (Rom. 7:18–25)

Yes, thanks be to God we do not need to be a slave to the pull of the carnal nature toward sin. We can live free in Christ as we come under the control of the Holy Spirit!

> For if you live according to the flesh, you will die; but if by the Spirit you put to death the misdeeds of the body, you will live. For those who are led by the Spirit of God are the children of God. (Rom. 8:13, 14)

It is absolutely imperative that we hear the voice of God in our minds, for unless our lives are governed by the principles of God's Word, the inner guidance of the Spirit, and His providential leading, we will surely go astray. The apostle Paul says that we must take every thought captive to make it obedient to Christ (2 Cor. 10:5)! If we would follow this advice, we would never depart from the will of God, for we would have a moment by moment living connection with Him.

"Make every effort to live in peace with everyone and to be holy; without holiness no one will see the Lord" (Heb. 12:14). This text is telling us that unless we are in agreement with God, we will not be among the redeemed. For those who fall asleep in Jesus, the records of their lives are judged in accordance with what they knew to be true of God's law, His character, and His requirements. No one is held responsible for what they did not know and had no opportunity to learn. But for those who live through the time of trouble without a mediator, their robes of character must be spotless, without guile, or retaining one lie from the evil one. Enoch is the Biblical example of such a person.

> How did Enoch walk with God? He educated his mind and heart to ever feel that he was in the presence of God, and when in perplexity his prayers would ascend to God to keep him. (*Last Day* Events, p. 71)

We can have what Enoch had. We can have Christ as our constant companion. Enoch walked with God, and when assailed by the tempter, he could talk with God about it. He had no 'It is written,' as we have, but he had a knowledge of his heavenly companion. He made God his Counsellor, and was closely bound up with Jesus. And Enoch was honored in this course. He was translated to heaven without seeing death. And those who will be translated at the close of time, will be those who commune with God on earth. Those who make manifest that their life is hid with Christ in God will ever be representing Him in all their life-practices. Selfishness will be cut out by the roots. (*The Seventh-day Adventist Bible Commentary*, vol. 1, p. 1087)

Because of our fallen nature, communing with God is not a natural experience for the human heart. We hear our own thoughts, the thoughts and ideas that others have expressed to us, and even the voices of evil spirits. Since our minds were created to be receptors of God's communications to us, we need to learn to distinguish between the voices that vie for our attention.

For thousands of years Satan has been experimenting upon the properties of the human mind, and he has learned to know it well. By his subtle workings in these last days he is linking the human mind with his own, imbuing it with his own thoughts; and he is doing this work in so deceptive a manner that those who accept his guidance know not that they are being led by him at his will. The great deceiver hopes so to confuse the minds of men and women that none but his voice will be heard. (*Medical Ministry*, p. 111)

There is not an impulse of our nature, not a faculty of the mind or an inclination of the heart, but needs to be, moment by moment, under the control of the Spirit of God. (*Messages to Young People*, p. 62)

We cannot for one moment separate ourselves from Christ with safety. (Ibid., p. 115)

Satan cannot touch the mind or intellect unless we yield it to him. (*The Seventh-day Adventist Bible Commentary*, vol. 6, p. 1105)

Satan finds in human hearts some point where he can gain a foothold; some sinful desire is cherished by means of which his temptations assert their power. (*The Seventh-day Adventist Bible Commentary*, vol. 7, p. 927)

Through defects in the character, Satan works to gain control of the whole mind, and he knows that if these defects are cherished, he will succeed. (*The Great Controversy 1888*, p. 489)

So, in addition to the temptations that come from our fallen human nature, we also have Satan, our enemy, using all his powers to lure us into sin. Therefore, God, in His great mercy, has provided for us a way of escape.

This "way" is the sanctuary, the place of safety from the great roaring lion, who walks about looking for someone to devour (see 1 Peter 5:8). If we avail ourselves of this wonderful gift, we will escape the wily deceptions of the evil one. God is now inviting us to open our hearts to study and understand the hidden insights in the earthly sanctuary service, which will prepare us to serve Him forever in the heavenly sanctuary above.

Chapter Five

Living in His Presence

Have you ever wondered what it would be like to always be in the presence of God, walking with Him, talking with Him, seeing His beautiful smile, basking in the radiance of His presence? I long for that day, for His very being emanates joy and love! But I have discovered that the earthly sanctuary was given as a pattern to teach us how to connect with God and live in His presence even now.

It is understood by many that our thoughts and feelings comprise the basic essence of who we are. Our thoughts and feelings not only affect our whole being but also radiate out into the lives of all who come into our presence.

> The influence of every man's thoughts and actions surrounds him like an invisible atmosphere, which is unconsciously breathed in by all who come in contact with him. (*Testimonies for the Church,* vol. 5, p. 111)

> Those who are brought in contact with us are affected for good or evil by our words and actions. We are unconsciously diffusing the fragrance of our character upon the moral atmosphere surrounding us

or we are poisoning that atmosphere by thoughts, words, and deeds which have a deleterious influence. (*In Heavenly Places*, p. 274)

Every soul is surrounded by an atmosphere of its own.... By the atmosphere surrounding us, every person with whom we come in contact is consciously or unconsciously affected. This is a responsibility from which we cannot free ourselves. Our words, our acts, our dress, our deportment, even the expression of the countenance, has an influence. Upon the impression thus made there hang results for good or evil which no man can measure.... And the wider the sphere of our influence, the more good we may do. (*Messages to Young People*, pp. 417, 418)

Purity of thought must be cherished as indispensable to the work of influencing others. There must be a pure, holy atmosphere surrounding the soul, an atmosphere that will tend to quicken the spiritual life of all who inhale it. (*Medical Ministry*, p. 206)

The faces of men and women who talk with God, to whom the invisible world is a reality, express the peace of God. They carry with them the soft and genial atmosphere of heaven, and diffuse it in deeds of kindness and words of love. (Ibid., p. 252)

It is the privilege of every worker first to talk with God in the secret place of prayer and then to talk with the people as God's mouthpiece. Men and women who commune with God, who have an abiding Christ, make the very atmosphere holy, because they are cooperating with holy angels. (*Testimonies for the Church*, vol. 6, p. 52)

Since communing with God is so important—in fact, absolutely necessary for a vibrant, productive, successful Christian life—it is imperative that we know how such a life is produced. The rest of this chapter is dedicated to introducing the sanctuary as God's way of communicating with Him. As David said, "Thy way, O God, is in the sanctuary" (Ps. 77:13, KJV). Jesus said, "Is it not written: 'My house will be called a house of prayer for all nations'?" (Mark 11:17). He was quoting from Isaiah 56:6, 7:

And foreigners who bind themselves to the LORD to minister to him ... and to be his servants, *all who keep the Sabbath without desecrating it and who hold fast to my covenant*—these I will bring to my holy mountain and give them joy in my house of prayer ... for my house will be called a house of prayer for all nations. (emphasis added)

Notice that the prerequisites for finding a deep relationship with God in His sanctuary are to keep His Sabbath and hold fast to His covenant. Several times in Scripture, God's law is called His "covenant of love." One of these is found in 1 Kings 8:23 in Solomon's prayer at the dedication of the temple: "Lord, the God of Israel, there is no God like you in heaven above or on earth below—you who keep your covenant of love with your servants who continue wholeheartedly in your way."

Why would God call His Ten Commandment law a "covenant of love"? Many people look at the law as being a yoke of bondage. It is common to hear Christians say that they are not under law, but under grace. Would the same persons want to live in a country where there were no laws to protect the citizens? God's law contains the instructions that govern all of His creation. Just as every new car is accompanied by an owner's manual that gives instructions for keeping the car in good running order, so God has given us instructions that keep us alive, happy, and in connection with Himself. Apart from His law, we self-destruct. We cannot break these laws without inviting eventual mental and physical disease and death. Imagine our heavenly Father's longing for His children to accept His invitation to join Him in this covenant of love! His heart yearns to see every one functioning within the circle of His protecting arms.

In every covenant there must be at least two parties. Each is responsible for fulfilling their side of the conditions, promises and terms of the covenant. Herein lies the problem with human obedience to God's law. As Paul states in Romans 8:7, "The mind governed by the flesh is hostile to God; it does not submit to God's law, nor can it do so. Those who are in the realm of the flesh cannot please God."

How are we going to change this carnal heart of ours to come into a loving, restful companionship with our heavenly Father? How can we be transformed in heart and mind to be a beloved friend of God like Abraham, Moses, Enoch, and Daniel? God has provided the way for us through the sanctuary. Each part of the sanctuary was designed to transform the worshipper from a child of earth to a child of heaven. Sadly, very few Israelites really understood the deeper meaning of the sanctuary service, and very few Christians understand it now. But this can all be changed as we study the sanctuary throughout the Bible, with the additional light shining from the New Testament, and also from the writings of Ellen White. Below are some quotations which will help to identify the earthly sanctuary as a representation of the very home of God.

> A glorious throne, exalted from the beginning, is the place of our sanctuary. (Jer. 17:12)

> There is a river whose streams make glad the city of God, the holy place where the Most High dwells. (Ps. 46:4)

> How lovely is your dwelling place, LORD Almighty! My soul yearns, even faints, for the courts of the LORD; my heart and my flesh cry out for the living God. (Ps. 84:1, 2)

> In the temple in heaven, the dwelling place of God, His throne is established in righteousness and judgment. (*The Great Controversy*, p. 415)

> The heavenly temple [is] the abiding place of the King of Kings. (*Patriarchs and Prophets*, p. 357)

God loves His children so much that He wants us to have access to His throne in heaven whenever we desire to connect with Him. Help is just a prayer away, and the heavenly sanctuary is open for all who wish to come and receive the blessings of salvation. But there are requirements for this privilege, and all who wish to enter the heavenly courts must obey them.

> Son of man, describe the temple to the people of Israel, that they may be ashamed of their sins. Let them consider the plan, and if they are ashamed of all they have done, make known to them the design of the temple—its arrangement, its exits and entrances—its whole design and all its regulations and laws. Write these down before them so that they may be faithful to its design and follow all its regulations. This is the law of the temple: All the surrounding area on top of the mountain will be most holy. Such is the law of the temple. (Ezek. 43:10–12)

> We all need to keep the subject of the sanctuary in mind…. There is a sanctuary in heaven, and … a pattern of this sanctuary was once built on this earth. God desires His people to become familiar with this pattern, keeping ever before their minds the heavenly sanctuary, where God is all and in all. (Lt. 233, 1904)

> I saw that everything in heaven was in perfect order…. Said the angel, 'Behold ye and know how perfect, how beautiful, the order in heaven; follow it.' (*Early Writings*, pp. xxx, xxxi)

Through the sacrifices and offerings brought to the earthly sanctuary, the children of Israel were to lay hold of the merits of a Saviour to come. And, in the wisdom of God the particulars of this work were given us that we might, by looking to them, understand the work of Jesus in the heavenly sanctuary. (Ibid., p. 253)

It is those who by faith follow Jesus in the great work of the atonement, who receive the benefits of His mediation in their behalf, while those who reject the light which brings to view this work of mediation are not benefitted thereby. (*The Great Controversy*, p. 430)

The temple of God is opened in heaven, and the threshold is flushed with the glory which is for every church that will love God and keep His commandments. We need to study, to meditate, and to pray. Then we will have spiritual eyesight to discern the inner courts of the celestial temple. (*Testimonies for the Church*, vol. 6, p. 368)

It seems clear from these statements that the earthly sanctuary was given to provide a way for fallen humanity to enter by faith and obedience into the heavenly sanctuary. I do not mean that we can earn salvation by ritualistic obedience or human effort, but the keys to recovery from the slavery of the sinful mind are found in the sanctuary, whereby we can once again be united with the holiness and purity of God through a relationship with Jesus.

"It was Christ who planned the arrangement for the first earthly tabernacle. He ... was the heavenly architect who marked out the plan for the sacred building where His name was to be honored" (*Christ's Object Lessons*, p. 349). Since the word "name" symbolizes the deeper meaning of "character," we can see how the sanctuary service was depicting the character of Christ, which, if understood and followed, would renew the mind into the image of Jesus. This is why the sanctuary was so holy, and why it was to be constructed with total perfection. Anything less would not exemplify the perfect character of Jesus, the spotless Lamb of God. It was also the reason Uzzah was smitten with death when touching the ark to stabilize it and keep it from falling. Jesus needed no human hand to prevent Him from falling. He relied wholly upon His Father.

This is the example for us as well. No human being is responsible for our salvation. It is true that we are to help one another along the pathway to heaven. But only Jesus can transfer His perfect character to us. Therefore, the sanctuary pathway has been made available to everyone who will avail him or herself of the principles of eternal life that are hidden therein. Let us look now at these profound, yet simple principles, which will lead not only to eternal life but will also prepare the final generation for the seal of God—the sign of God's approval.

Chapter 6

Journey to the Throne

The first step in this sacred journey is found in one of the Psalms of David: "Enter his gates with thanksgiving and his courts with praise; give thanks to him and praise his name. For the LORD is good and his love endures forever; his faithfulness continues through all generations" (Ps. 100:4, 5). To many people, the first step in connecting with God is to bring all their sins, sorrows, burdens, and agitations to God with heaviness of heart. While it is true that God hears every sincere prayer and works to bring us relief, the question is this: while we are in such a negative state of mind, will we be able to hear His voice of comfort and counsel? He longs to do so much more for us than just relieve our immediate problems. He allows trial so that He can teach us about things we need to learn in order to be overcomers and live in the light of His eternal presence without guile. But like Mary Magdalene in the Garden of Gethsemane, we weep with sorrow over some difficulty we are having, without perceiving that Jesus is right beside us and would gladly carry our burdens if we would simply accept the victory and joy that He wants to give us.

I will always remember the day that I was kneeling beside my desk with my head buried in the chair, weeping because of some problem I was experiencing. Suddenly, like a bolt of lightning, the realization came to me that Jesus was right there with me, and the solution to my problem was only waiting for me to claim it by faith. My feelings immediately changed from gloom and grief to joy, peace, and praise. It was my first step in learning that in order to connect with all the promised blessings that God has for me, I must follow the sanctuary prescription of coming into His courts—or connecting with His presence—through praise and thanksgiving for all of His wonderful blessings to me.

But the steps in the sanctuary are not just an outline to follow in our prayer time. Remember—the sanctuary exemplifies the character of Jesus at all times and in all situations. Jesus never succumbed to depression, criticism, bitterness, lust, pride, gossip, or any of the other human reactions to our earthly condition. He was ever praising and trusting of His heavenly Father, and He walked in His moment-by-moment instructions, counsel, and guidance. He was always in connection with His Father, and we can be, too. Disconnection from Him means that we will certainly give in to the impulses of the fleshly nature. We often hear that we should put on the robe of Christ's righteousness. Some think that it is something we put on over our own sinful so that God will look at His Son and not us, but the robe of Christ's righteousness is also very practical and visible to others. Notice this amazing statement by Ellen White: "The day is coming in which the battle will have been fought, the victory won.... All will be a happy, united family, clothed with the garments of praise and thanksgiving—the robe of Christ's righteousness" (*Testimonies for the Church*, vol. 8, p. 42).

So when we put on the robe of Christ's righteousness—His character—others will see in us the same love Jesus had for others, His cheerfulness and patience in the face of trial, His forbearance with the faults of those with whom He associated, and His ministry to the suffering. In short, they will see the life of Jesus being lived out in us! Praising God means more than words; it means more than music. It means letting Jesus work through our hands, our voices, our lives, bringing praise and honor to God for His gracious gift of salvation and for a place to serve Him in His kingdom, both here and in the hereafter.

Once we have put on the garment of praise, we are ready to yield ourselves to God completely and die to every selfish thought and impulse. This is exemplified by the altar of sacrifice, which was the first item of furniture in the courtyard of the sanctuary. This altar was made of brass and was the place where worshippers confessed their sins over the head of an animal that represented the Savior, who was to come and die for them. This provision was not to enable the worshipper to feel comfortable in continuing the cycle of sinning and repenting, but to see the devastating effect that sin has in leading to the death of the substitute, and eventually of oneself. It was meant to teach the sinner to go the full route of the sanctuary and be cleansed of even the desire to sin.

It is this carnal desire that must die in the fully converted heart. This is exemplified by the horns on the altar. These horns were placed on each of the four corners of the altar. They were to be made of the same substance as the altar itself (see Exod. 38:2). The symbolism of this is very important. It is mentioned in Jeremiah 17:1: "Judah's sin is engraved with an iron tool, inscribed with a flint point, on the tablets of their hearts and on the horns of their altars." The analogy used here in identifying the horns of the altars as being the place where sin is found has deep meaning for each of us.

The word "horn" in the Bible means strength, status, or power. It comes from the concept of horns used by male animals for aggression or to defend themselves or the herd of females and young ones. Thus, the horns protruding upward and outward on the altar symbolized the human heart's desire or urge to protect one's self or to be aggressive in a carnal way. The priest was to dip his finger in the blood of the slain animal and place some on each of the four horns of the altar. This would indicate that the carnal urges of the natural heart would be changed into the beautiful character of the Lamb of God. In place of self-protection, the total dependence of Jesus upon His Father would appear in the daily life.

> We are in the day of God's preparation. Let nothing be regarded as of sufficient worth to draw your minds from the work of preparing for the great day of judgment. Get ready. Let not cold unbelief hold your souls away from God, but let His love burn on the altar of your hearts. (*Testimonies for the Church*, vol. 5, p. 590)

However, according to Jeremiah 17:1, sin is not only engraved upon the horns of the altar but also upon the tablets of the heart. This is a fascinating and important concept! The word, "tablet," is the same Hebrew word as the tablets of stone upon which were engraved the law of God that were kept in the ark of the covenant in the most holy place of the sanctuary. This is the same "covenant of love" that was mentioned in chapter five of this book. In the Hebrew language, the word for "heart" means: the inner person, self, the seat of thought and emotion. Symbolically speaking, the law of God must be kept in the innermost part of the mind, emotions, and conscience, thus controlling the whole person. Otherwise, the law of sin, selfishness, and death will rule the life and become as hardened as stone. A person with a stony heart can only be changed by a miracle of grace, an act of God, which is freely performed for anyone who truly desires to become His obedient child.

"I will give them an undivided heart and put a new spirit in them; I will remove from them their heart of stone and give them a heart of flesh. Then they will follow my decrees and be careful to keep my laws. They will be my people, and I will be their God" (Ezek. 11:19, 20). The sanctuary is all about heart work. The stony heart of selfishness must be exchanged for a heart that is malleable by the Holy Spirit. God wants to talk to us, work with us, reason with us.

> 'Come now, let us settle the matter,' says the LORD. 'Though your sins be like scarlet, they shall be as white as snow; though they are red as crimson, they shall be like wool. If you are willing and obedient, you will eat the good things of the land; but if you resist and rebel, you will be devoured by the sword.' For the mouth of the LORD has spoken. (Isa. 1:18–20)

Can you imagine the incredible love and longing God has for each of His children, and how much He wants to have a relationship with us, talk with us, and teach us all the mysteries of salvation which would keep us from destroying ourselves? He tries every means possible to guide us into safe paths, but so often we go our own way, disregard God's counsel, follow our feelings, and end up hurting ourselves and others. Therefore, God is always calling us to come back, repent, and be healed of the wounds sin has brought upon us.

> Yet the Israelites says, 'The way of the Lord is not just.' Are my ways unjust, people of Israel? Is it not your ways that are unjust? Therefore, you Israelites, I will judge each of you according to your own ways, declares the Sovereign LORD. Repent! Turn away from all your offenses; then sin will not be your downfall. Rid yourselves of all the offenses you have committed, and get a new heart and a new spirit. Why will you die, people of Israel? For I take no pleasure in the death of anyone, declares the Sovereign LORD. Repent and live! (Ezek. 18:29–32)

I love God so much for His mercy and patience! Time and time again we fail Him, but He holds out His arms to us and welcomes us back into safety and peace and fellowship with Him. I am learning more and more as I keep close to Him in the sanctuary; I do not have to wander away from His side. I listen for His voice moment by moment, and "He guides me along the right paths for his name's sake" (Ps. 23:3). I do not want to leave Him anymore. I want to keep self on the altar and Jesus always on the throne of my heart, don't you?

Another very important function of the altar of sacrifice is that this is the place in our prayer where we give all our burdens to Jesus. Sin of any kind is certainly a burden upon the soul. But there are many other burdens and worries that weigh us down and sap our energies and life forces. Finances, relationships, health issues, family problems—the list could go on about the challenges that face us each day. These we must give to Jesus and allow Him to carry the heaviest part of the load.

> Humble yourselves, therefore, under God's mighty hand, that he may lift you up in due time. Cast all your anxiety on him because he cares for you. (1 Peter 5:6, 7)

> Do not be anxious about anything, but in everything, by prayer and petition, with thanksgiving, present your requests to God. And the peace of God, which transcends all understanding, will guard your hearts and your minds in Christ Jesus. (Phil. 4:6, 7)

> Cast your cares on the LORD and he will sustain you; he will never let the righteous be shaken. (Ps. 55:22)

> Our heavenly Father has the power of turning the flinty rock into life-giving and refreshing streams. We shall never know, until we are face to face with God, ... how many burdens He has borne for us, and how many burdens He would have been glad to bear if, with childlike faith, we had brought them to Him. (*Reflecting Christ*, p. 353)

> In being co-workers with Christ in the great work for which He gave His life, we shall find true rest.... Wearing this yoke keeps you near the side of Christ, and *He bears the heaviest part of the load*.... Rest comes to them in the consciousness that they are trying to please the Lord. (*The Seventh-day Adventist Bible Commentary*, vol. 5, p. 1090, emphasis added)

What a blessed privilege it is to walk with Jesus every moment of the day and know that He—our dearest Friend—has all the answers to our problems, and that He can, and will, work out everything for His glory!

Chapter Seven

The Sword and the Spirit

In the courtyard of the earthly sanctuary, there were two articles of furniture: the altar of sacrifice and the laver, which was a basin for washing. We have already considered the altar and have seen the personal application of self-surrender and dying with Christ to our sinful urges and practices. It is also symbolic of giving all our burdens to Jesus and letting Him carry them for us, working everything out according to His miraculous ways of solving even the most difficult situations. We can now go on to the laver, which was located between the altar and the curtain that surrounded the holy and most holy places. It was at the laver that the priest washed the blood and soil from his hands and feet before entering the sacred precincts. There is an even deeper, more spiritual purpose for the laver, which is found in Ephesians 5:25–27:

> Husbands, love your wives, just as Christ loved the church and gave himself up for her to make her holy, *cleansing her by the washing with water through the word,* and to present her to himself as a radiant

church, without stain or wrinkle or any other blemish, but holy and blameless. (emphasis added)

When we first begin our Christian walk, our minds are filled with the principles of the world and the flesh by which we have guided our lives. But after we surrender our hearts to Jesus, a complete change must take place. It is by the study and application of the Word of God that our sins are washed away, and we are prepared to receive the infilling of the Spirit of God! Old habits and concepts must give way to the instructions found in Scripture. It is the Holy Spirit Himself who is the Author of the Bible. Using holy men of God who listened to His voice and wrote down what He revealed to them, the Holy Spirit now attends the reading of the word and speaks to the heart of each person who opens the Bible with a sincere heart, seeking for truth.

The enemy of our souls is ever trying to find ways to cleverly subvert our minds so that we will accept His deceptions. When Jesus was in the wilderness of temptation, He did not parley with the devil. He immediately met Him with the truths contained in the Scriptures. We must do the same if we expect to be successful in the battle with the evil one. Satan was not permitted to come to Jesus until He had spent forty days alone, communing with His Father. Likewise, we cannot hope to defeat the devil if we do not spend time alone with Jesus, communing with Him, learning from Him through the Scriptures and the enlightenment of the Holy Spirit.

> If you come to the study of the Scriptures in humility, with earnest prayer for guidance, angels of God will open to you its living realities; and if you cherish the precepts of truth, they will be to you as a wall of fire against the temptations, delusions, and enchantments of Satan. (*Our High Calling*, p. 210)

> The Holy Spirit is beside every true searcher of God's Word, enabling him to discover the hidden gems of truth. Divine illumination comes to his mind, stamping the truth upon him with a new, fresh importance. He is filled with a joy never before felt. The peace of God rests upon him. The preciousness of truth is realized as never before. A heavenly light shines upon the Word, making it appear as though every letter were tinged with gold. God Himself speaks to the heart, making His Word spirit and life. (*Reflecting Christ*, p. 128)

> The Holy Spirit is in the Word of God.... The precious Word of God is a solid foundation upon which to build.... Here is presented before us a rich banquet, of which all who believe in Christ as a personal Saviour may eat. He is the Tree of life to all who continue to

feed on Him.... All who study these precious utterances may have strong consolation. If they will feed upon the banquet of God's Word, they will gain an experience of the highest value.... The banquet is spread before us; we are invited to eat the Word of God, which will strengthen spiritual muscle and sinew. (*This Day With God*, p. 292)

One of the most wonderful experiences we can have while studying the Scriptures is to find that God is speaking directly to us, going down deep into our souls, answering our questions and giving us counsel and instruction, which we often recognize as being the very thing we need at that time. "For the word of God is alive and active. Sharper than any double-edged sword, it penetrates even to dividing soul and spirit, joints and marrow; it judges the thoughts and attitudes of the heart" (Heb. 4:12).

All this is to prepare our hearts for receiving the Holy Spirit in full measure, which is represented by the seven-branched candlestick, located on the left side of the Holy Place. Perhaps now we can understand why the first three steps in the sanctuary are so important. In order to receive the fruit of the Spirit, we must be cleansed from the thoughts and feelings of the sinful mind.

> The acts of the flesh are obvious: sexual immorality, impurity and debauchery; idolatry and witchcraft; hatred, discord, jealousy, fits of rage, selfish ambition, dissensions, factions and envy; drunkenness, orgies, and the like. I warn you, as I did before, that those who live like this will not inherit the kingdom of God. But the fruit of the Spirit is love, joy, peace, forbearance, kindness, goodness, faithfulness, gentleness and self-control. Against such things there is no law. Those who belong to Christ Jesus have crucified the flesh with its passions and desires. Since we live by the Spirit, let us keep in step with the Spirit. (Gal. 5:19–25)

Many Christians feel they can live like the world, think like the world, indulge in the pleasures of the world, and still receive the blessings of the Spirit of God. This is a deception. If we wish to have a vibrant, fulfilling, and victorious Christian life, we must follow God's prescription for spiritual health, which is outlined for us in the sanctuary. This must be a daily, moment by moment experience. The sanctuary is not just prayer, but a way of life that prepares us to be at home in the presence of God.

There are two more articles of furniture in the holy place. On the right side is the table of showbread. This represents the life of Jesus, lived out for us, which we can—and must—partake of in order to represent Him to those around us. Jesus said:

> I am the bread of life.... I am the living bread that came down from heaven. Whoever eats this bread will live forever.... Very truly I tell you, unless you eat the flesh of the Son of Man and drink his blood, you have no life in you. Whoever eats my flesh and drinks my blood has eternal life, and I will raise him up at the last day.... Just as the living Father sent me and I live because of the Father, so the one who feeds on me will live because of me. (John 6:48–57)

When the disciples began to grumble among themselves because of the strange words that Jesus had spoken, Jesus explained to them the true meaning of His words. "The Spirit gives life; the flesh counts for nothing. The words I have spoken to you—they are full of the Spirit and life" (John 6:63).

Jesus was filled by the Holy Spirit from the moment of His conception and throughout His life on earth. The Spirit was the method of communication by which Father and Son were linked together. Of course, the Father, the Son, and the Holy Spirit were always one with each other throughout eternity, but the Spirit had a very special role in the earthly life of Jesus. In taking upon Himself the body of fallen man, Jesus needed the constant communication between Himself and His Father, which was provided by the Spirit. This kept His mind pure, holy, and undefiled. Thus, He could say of Himself: "I do nothing on my own but speak just what the Father has taught me. The one who sent me is with me; he has not left me alone, for I always do what pleases him" (John 8:28, 29).

> What would our lives be like if we, too, could say, "I do nothing on my own but speak just what the Father has taught me"? But isn't this exactly what the life of Jesus is teaching us? If we eat His flesh and drink His blood, are we not saying that we are to live the life that He lived? Can we consult with ourselves or others and find the life of perfect obedience that Jesus displayed? No, a thousand times, no! We, too, must be connected continually with heaven through the Holy Spirit, who brings the life of Jesus—His thoughts and feelings and teachings—and implants these in our hearts! What a glorious privilege we have of eating His flesh, drinking His blood, living His life!

> We have been called to the knowledge of Christ, and that is to the knowledge of glory and virtue. It is a knowledge of the perfection of

the divine character, manifested to us in Jesus Christ, that opens up to us communion with God.... Scarcely can the human mind comprehend what is the breadth and depth and height of the spiritual attainments that can be reached by becoming partakers of the divine nature.... Christ must be all in all to us; He must dwell in the heart; His life must circulate through us, as the blood circulates through the veins. His Spirit must be a vitalizing power that will cause us to influence others to become Christlike and holy. (*Our High Calling*, p. 60)

God must be ever in our thoughts. We must hold converse Him while we walk by the way, and while our hands are engaged in labor. In all the purposes and pursuits of life we must inquire, What will the Lord have me to do? How shall I please Him who has given His life a ransom for me? Thus may we walk with God, as did Enoch of old; and ours may be the testimony which he received, that he pleased God. (Ibid., p. 61)

The union with Christ, once formed, must be maintained.... This is no casual touch, no off-and-on connection. The branch becomes a part of the living vine. The communication of life, strength, and fruitfulness from the root to the branches is unobstructed and constant. Separated from the vine, the branch cannot live. No more, said Jesus, can you live apart from Me. The life you have received from Me can be preserved only by continual communication. Without Me you cannot overcome one sin, or resist one temptation ... The channel of communication must be open continually between man and his God.... Cling to Jesus, and receive from Him the strength and perfection of His own character. (*The Desire of Ages*, p. 676)

It is only by personal union with Christ, by communion with Him daily, hourly, that we can bear the fruits of the Holy Spirit.... Our growth in grace, our joy, our usefulness, all depend on our union with Christ and the degree of faith we exercise in Him. (*Sons and Daughters of God*, p. 290)

Does the requirement of continual union with Christ seem like an impossibility? If we indulge in the entertainment and ways of the world around us, we certainly will be tainted by the thoughts, feelings, and attitudes of whatever we put into our minds. Our only hope is to give up anything that would separate us from the closest relationship with Jesus that is possible. This is why Paul instructs us to "take captive every thought to make it obedient to Christ" (2 Cor. 10:5). It is only then that we will experience the joyful union with Him that is available to every Christian! It is this experience that prepares us to enter into the next phase of the sanctuary—communing with God at the altar of incense, and finally, entering the Most Holy Place, where the cleansing of our souls is completed.

Chapter Eight
The Urim and Thummim

It should be quite clear by now that the sanctuary is a place of restored communion with God. Before Adam and Eve sinned, they had open communication with their Creator, but sin separated the human race from this privilege. The tempter now has constant access to our minds, and only by following God's pathway back into harmony with Him can the relationship be restored. Through the rudimentary sacrificial system established outside the gate of the Garden of Eden, the first principles of the sanctuary service were revealed. Later these principles were greatly expanded to Moses on Mt. Sinai. The Israelite nation, as God's specially chosen people, were privileged to set up the sacred service that guides us all the way to the coming of Jesus.

We have now covered briefly the first five steps of the sanctuary, which enables the fallen human mind to reestablish communication with the perfect mind of God. One basic principle behind all the aspects of the sanctuary is to bring us back into harmony with God's principles of love and mental health.

God has commanded us, 'Be ye holy; for I am holy;' and an inspired apostle declares that without holiness 'no man shall see the Lord.' Holiness is agreement with God. By sin the image of God in man has been marred and well-nigh obliterated; it is the work of the gospel to restore that which has been lost; and we are to cooperate with the divine agency in this work. And how can we come into harmony with God, how shall we receive His likeness, unless we obtain a knowledge of Him? It is this knowledge that Christ came into the world to reveal unto us. (*Testimonies for the Church*, vol. 5, p. 743)

Before Jesus came into the world, humankind had no direct knowledge of Him. The sanctuary was to help give a visible revelation of the character of Christ. Once the meaning of these symbols were learned, the diligent student was now capable of connecting with God again. It would be well to spell these out in a little review before going on to the last two items.

First, the exercise of true, heartfelt praise lifts one's mind into the very courts of heaven, where there is constant praise and joyful singing around the throne of God. It has been discovered that every person has a mental and emotional "set point," which is the most common way we think about life. If a person has learned to have a low set point, he or she will level out at that point no matter how many times something good happens in his life. Eventually, his or her mood and thinking will return to the habit of depressed thinking. Conversely, if a person has a high set point, no matter how many bad things happen in his or her life, he or she will bounce back and level out at his or her normal pleasant and cheerful attitude. Fortunately, the set point can be reeducated, and the sanctuary is designed to help us see every experience in our lives through the attitude of praise and thanksgiving to God.

The second item of the sanctuary—the altar of sacrifice—helps us to identify with and assimilate the humility of Christ. We are naturally inward focused, looking at our own feelings about ourselves and others. We tend to be critical and to complain when things don't go as we wish they would, but Jesus invites us to lay all our cares and fears down at His feet and leave them there. Then we can be free to rejoice in the Lord and minister to others with a heart free from the burdens that would otherwise crush out our happiness and usefulness.

Next, the laver reminds us that our minds must be brought into harmony with God's principles through His Word. Washed from error and selfishness, we are then ready for the outpouring and empowering of the Holy Spirit, bringing His gifts and graces to us. Finally, the table of showbread points us to an intimate relationship with Jesus as our only way to have His righteousness shining out from us to others.

> Study carefully the divine-human character, and constantly inquire, 'What would Jesus do were He in my place?' This should be the measurement of our duty. (*Ministry of Healing*, p. 491)

> He is to be consulted in all things as to how the powers of your mind and the affections of your heart shall be employed. (*That I May Know Him*, p. 135)

At this point, we are ready to move on to the golden altar of incense, which stood before the inner curtain that veiled the Most Holy Place. From this altar, the prayers of God's people would ascend. It represents the method of communication that is provided for everyone who desires to have access to the heart of God.

> Another angel, who had a golden censer, came and stood at the altar. He was given much incense to offer, with the prayers of all God's people, on the golden altar in front of the throne. The smoke of the incense, together with the prayers of God's people, went up before God from the angel's hand. (Rev. 8:3, 4)

> In the offering of incense the priest was brought more directly into the presence of God than in any other act of the daily ministration.... As in that typical service the priest looked by faith to the mercy seat which he could not see, so the people of God are now to direct their prayers to Christ, their great High Priest, who, unseen by human vision, is pleading in their behalf in the sanctuary above. (*Patriarchs and Prophets*, p. 353)

> Morning and evening the heavenly universe behold every household that prays, and the angel with the incense, representing the blood of the atonement, finds access to God. (*The Seventh-day Adventist Bible Commentary*, vol. 7, p. 971)

Finally, we come to the last compartment of the sanctuary, the holy of holies, in which the ark of the covenant containing the sacred law of God was placed. The cover of the ark was called the mercy seat. It was here that God communicated with the priest in behalf of His people.

> Above the mercy seat was the Shekinah, the manifestation of the divine Presence; and from between the cherubim, God made known

his will. Divine messages were sometimes communicated to the high priest by a voice from the cloud. Sometimes a light fell upon the angel at the right, to signify approval or acceptance, or a shadow or cloud rested upon the one at the left to reveal disapproval or rejection. (*Patriarchs and Prophets*, p. 349)

There was also another method of communication that God provided through the breastplate worn by the high priest. Upon this breastplate were twelve precious stones set in gold, and each was engraved with one of the names of the twelve tribes of Israel. There were also two precious stones that were used to discern the will of God.

At the right and left of the breastplate were two large stones of great brilliancy. These were known as the Urim and Thummim. By them the will of God was made known through the high priest. When questions were brought for decision before the Lord, a halo of light encircling the precious stone at the right was a token of the divine consent or approval, while a cloud shadowing the stone at the left was an evidence of denial or disapprobation. (Ibid., p. 351)

Whenever Aaron enters the Holy Place, he will bear the names of the sons of Israel over his heart on the breastpiece of decision as a continuing memorial before the LORD. Also put the Urim and the Thummim in the breastpiece, so they may be over Aaron's heart whenever he enters the presence of the LORD. Thus Aaron will always bear the means of making decisions for the Israelites over his heart before the LORD. (Exod. 28:29, 30)

Don't you wish that we could have a Urim and Thummim available to us today so we could ask God all the questions we need to know for our daily lives? But, dear friends, that is exactly what God wants us to have through a knowledge of the sanctuary service. "Not only the sanctuary itself, but the ministration of the priests, was to 'serve unto the example and shadow of heavenly things'" (*Patriarchs and Prophets*, pp. 351, 352).

Let's take a little deeper look at the Urim and Thummim. "These words mean, respectively, 'light' and 'perfection'" (*The Seventh-day Adventist Bible Commentary*, vol. 1, p. 649). Remember that God also used a similar way of communicating in the Most Holy Place. For "yes," a light shone down upon the angel on the right side, which was located over the mercy seat. For "no," a cloud appeared over the angel on the left side. When I first tried to understand the significance of these two words, I could readily understand that a light would mean, "yes." But what would a cloud over perfection indicate?

Then it came became clear. The cloud indicated that the answer was "no" because it wasn't the perfect way. There is nothing imperfect in the sanctuary. Thus, for anything imperfect, the answer would be, "no."

God has placed in the brain of every person the ability to sense light and darkness. That is why we are told:

> Walk while you have the light, before darkness overtakes you. Whoever walks in the dark does not know where they are going. Believe in the light while you have it, so that you may become children of light. (John 12:35, 36)

> God is light; in him there is no darkness at all. If we claim to have fellowship with him and yet walk in the darkness, we lie and do not live by the truth. But if we walk in the light, as he is in the light, we have fellowship with one another, and the blood of Jesus, his Son, purifies us from all sin. (1 John 1:5–7)

In other words, if we look to Jesus all the time and focus our eyes of faith upon Him, He will have our constant attention and submission to His will. He can then cleanse us of everything that is imperfect.

> While pride, variance, and strife for supremacy are cherished, the heart cannot enter into fellowship with Christ. (*The Desire of Ages*, p. 650)

> Yielding to temptation begins in permitting the mind to waver, to be inconsistent in your trust in God. (*Thoughts From the Mount of Blessing*, p. 92)

> We cannot for one moment separate ourselves from Christ with safety. (*Messages to Young People*, p. 115)

> It is through the medium of His Spirit that God works upon the human heart; and when men willfully reject the Spirit and declare it to be from Satan, they cut off the channel by which God can communicate with them. By denying the evidence which God has been pleased to give them, they shut out the light which had been shining in their hearts, and as the result they are left in darkness. Thus the words of Christ are verified: 'If therefore the light that is in thee be darkness, how great is that darkness!' (*Testimonies for the Church*, vol. 5, p. 634)

As we look unto Jesus, all our lives will be aglow with that wondrous light. Every part of us is to be light; then whichever way we turn, light will be reflected from us to others. Christ is the way, the truth, and the life. In Him is no darkness at all; therefore, if we are in Christ, there will be no darkness in us. (*In Heavenly Places*, p. 281)

I have heard many people say, "God doesn't talk to me." I have also had the privilege of helping many to learn how to perceive the way God speaks to us. It comes from the principles of the sanctuary by which God speaks through His word, and through the tender impressions upon the heart and the mind by the still, small voice of the Holy Spirit. Dear Reader, if you do not know how to recognize the voice of God speaking to you through His appointed methods, please take the time and effort to learn. Do not rest satisfied with a superficial walk with Jesus. He longs for you to get to know Him personally and intimately. Your spiritual life will then be able to grow into a deep and satisfying relationship that is accessible to every Christian through the lessons found in the sanctuary!

Chapter Nine

Cleansing Heaven's Records

Every year at the end of the cycle of Jewish feast days, the most important feast of all was celebrated. This special high day was the Day of Atonement, when all the sins of Israel were ceremonially blotted out. What a joyous day it was for every child of Abraham when the solemn day of heart searching and repentance was over, and the sense of relief and freedom from past sins was realized.

> This is to be a lasting ordinance for you: On the tenth day of the seventh month you must deny yourselves and not do any work—whether native-born or a foreigner residing among you—because on this day atonement will be made for you, to cleanse you. Then, before the LORD, you will be clean from all your sins. (Lev. 16:29, 30)

Denying themselves meant, in this case, to fast. Notice also that the instructions for this feast day stated that this was to be a "lasting ordinance," meaning that this was something they would be required to do "for ever," as is stated in the King James Version. Although the observance of the Jewish feast days came to an end when Jesus became the slain Lamb who paid the ransom for everyone, the truths taught by the earthly sanctuary have now been transferred to Christ's work in the heavenly sanctuary.

> As the typical cleansing of the earthly was accomplished by the removal of the sins by which it had been polluted, so the actual cleansing of the heavenly is to be accomplished by the removal, or blotting out, of the sins which are there recorded. But before this can be accomplished, there must be an examination of the books of record to determine who, through repentance of sin and faith in Christ, are entitled to the benefits of His atonement. The cleansing of the sanctuary therefore involves a work of investigation—a work of judgment. (*The Great Controversy*, pp. 421, 422)

> The work of the investigative judgment and the blotting out of sins is to be accomplished before the second advent of the Lord. Since the dead are to be judged out of the things written in the books, it is impossible that the sins of men should be blotted out until after the judgment at which their cases are to be investigated.... When the investigative judgment closes, Christ will come, and His reward will be with Him to give to every man as his work shall be. (Ibid., p. 485)

> Those who would share the benefits of the Saviour's mediation should permit nothing to interfere with their duty to perfect holiness in the fear of God.... The subject of the sanctuary and the investigative judgment should be clearly understood by the people of God. All need a knowledge for themselves of the position and work of their great High Priest. Otherwise it will be impossible for them to exercise the faith which is essential at this time, or to occupy the position which God designs them to fill. (Ibid., p. 488)

> We are now living in the great day of atonement. In the typical service, while the high priest was making the atonement for Israel, all were required to afflict their souls by repentance of sin and humiliation before the Lord, lest they be cut off from among the people. In like manner, all who would have their names retained in the book of life, should now, in the few remaining days of their probation, afflict their souls before God by sorrow for sin, and true repentance. There must be deep, faithful searching of heart.... The Judgment is now passing in the sanctuary above. For more than forty years this work has been in progress. Soon—none know how soon—it will pass to the cases of the living. In the awful presence of God our lives are to come up in review. At this time above all others it behooves

every soul to heed the Saviour's admonition, 'Watch and pray; for ye know not when the time is.' [Mark 13:33.] 'If therefore thou shalt not watch, I will come on thee as a thief, and thou shalt not know what hour I will come upon thee.' [Revelation 3:3.] (*The Great Controversy 1888*, p. 490)

Much speculation about the meaning of these words has been made since they were written by Ellen White in the late 1800s. It has been understood and taught that when Jesus comes, we will be unaware of it and will not find out what His decision has been in our case until probation closes. This is when we will either stand with the company of the saved or receive the plagues and are lost. This erroneous belief has been terrifying for many of our dear people, for most of us see that we still have areas in our lives that need improvement and that we sometimes fall prey to our human weaknesses. Because of this, many believers have sought for other ways of seeing the concept of the judgment.

The most popular belief today seems to be that we are covered by grace, and if we have accepted Jesus as our Savior, we have nothing to fear in the judgment, or that we don't even come into judgment at all. This may seem very comforting, but is it true? Remember that in the earthly sanctuary, ALL were required to participate in the Day of Atonement services. Everyone had to fast and search their hearts to see if there was anything out of harmony with God's law. Anyone who did not comply with these requirements was cut off from his people (see Lev. 23:29).

Since we are now in the antitypical day of atonement—that is, the time in history when our great High Priest is cleansing the heavenly sanctuary of the sins of His people—what are the implications of the requirements for us if we expect our names to be retained in the Lamb's book of life? Doesn't it mean that we must cooperate with Jesus and allow Him to remove every stain of sin, including our thoughts, feelings, motives, words, and behavior? Shouldn't we attempt to reflect His life to all around us through the power of His indwelling Spirit? Do you believe that He can do this in you? If so, you will have the privilege of being prepared by Jesus to go through the time of trouble such as never was upon the earth until then. You will be among those who stand on Mt. Zion with the Lamb!

> The work of judgment which began in 1844, must continue until the cases of all are decided, both of the living and the dead; hence it will extend to the close of human probation. (Ibid., p. 436)

Those who are living upon the earth when the intercession of Christ shall cease in the sanctuary above, are to stand in the sight of a holy God without a mediator. Their robes must be spotless, their characters must be purified from sin by the blood of sprinkling. Through the grace of God and their own diligent effort, they must be conquerors in the battle with evil. While the investigative Judgment is going forward in Heaven, while the sins of penitent believers are being removed from the sanctuary, there is to be a special work of purification, of putting away of sin, among God's people upon earth.... When this work shall have been accomplished, the followers of Christ will be ready for his appearing. (Ibid., p. 425)

It is this "special work of purification" that is largely ignored or misunderstood by God's people today. Recently, I heard a well-known speaker give a moving sermon about the nearness of Christ's coming, especially in light of current events. He spoke of the possibility of the passing of the Sunday law, and stated that when this happens, we can know for certain that the judgment of the living has begun, since this is the final test for the people of God. But as solemn as this thought may be, he quickly gave comfort to his listeners by assuring them that if they have given their lives to Jesus, they have nothing to fear, for the blood of Jesus covers their sins, and when the Father looks at them He does not see them, but He sees His Son's perfect righteousness.

Personally, I am concerned for the many people who believe this so innocently and completely that they ignore the plain teaching of both the Scriptures and the Spirit of Prophecy concerning the preparation that is necessary to stand before God without a mediator. Notice these words of warning found in Malachi 3:1–5:

> 'I will send my messenger, who will prepare the way before me. Then suddenly the Lord you are seeking will come to his temple; the messenger of the covenant, whom you desire, will come,' says the LORD Almighty. But who can endure the day of his coming? Who can stand when he appears? For he will be like a refiner's fire or a launderer's soap. He will sit as a refiner and purifier of silver; he will purify the Levites and refine them like gold and silver. Then the LORD will have men who will bring offerings in righteousness, and the offerings of Judah and Jerusalem will be acceptable to the LORD, as in days gone by, as in former years. 'So I will come to put you on trial.... But do not fear me,' says the LORD Almighty.

This describes a purifying process, just as did the quotation taken earlier from *The Great Controversy 1888*, p. 425. What is needed is not just a pronouncement of a state of holiness, but a process by which holiness is produced in the life of the believer. And what is holiness? "Holiness is agreement with God" (*Testimonies for the Church*, vol. 5, p. 743).

Yes, agreement with God on everything—how we eat, how we dress, how we talk, how we feel, how we act, how we think. Does such a state come easily and naturally to any of us? Absolutely not! Our carnal nature is naturally hostile to God (see Rom. 8:7). How, then, can we ever come to a state of mind where we agree with God on everything? Paul tells us that this process is going to take effort!

> Make every effort to live in peace with everyone and to be holy; without holiness no one will see the Lord. (Heb. 12:14)

> We demolish arguments and every pretension that sets itself up against the knowledge of God, and we take captive every thought to make it obedient to Christ. (2 Cor. 10:5)

But, you may say, this has been the admonition to every Christian since New Testament times. What, then, is unique about the experience of those who will be cleansed just before Jesus comes? Dear Reader, continue on, for the next chapter will address this question specifically.

Chapter Ten

The Judgment of the Living

As I mentioned in the previous chapter, the subject of the judgment of the living is greatly misunderstood by most people. Some think it is a secret process performed by Jesus in the second apartment work in the heavenly sanctuary, and that His people will not know the verdict until after the close of probation, and it is too late. There is a sense in which this can be true. For review and clarification, let's look at these pivotal passages in *The Great Controversy 1888*:

> 'Watch ye therefore; ... lest coming suddenly He find you sleeping.' [Mark 13:35, 36.] Perilous is the condition of those who, growing weary of their watch, turn to the attractions of the world. While the man of business is absorbed in the pursuit of gain, while the pleasure-lover is seeking indulgence, while the daughter of fashion is arranging her adornments,—it may be in that hour the Judge of all the earth will pronounce the sentence, 'Thou art weighed in the balances, and art found wanting.' (p. 491)

Notice that the admonition of Jesus is to watch and pray, lest when He comes, He will find us sleeping. How similar this is to the disciples' experience in Gethsemane on the night of Jesus' arrest and trial before Pilate. He said to them, "Watch and pray so that you will not fall into temptation" (Matt. 26:41), but His warnings went unheeded. What a difference it would have made if the disciples had spent that time in prayer, as Jesus pleaded for them to do. What a blessing they could have been to Jesus in His hour of agony! And they would have been strengthened and prepared for the trying hours before them.

And now that we are on the very verge of the coming of Jesus and the great trial and tribulation that precedes His coming, how many of His followers are awake and actively preparing for the momentous events that are just before us? It is my observation that many sincerely believe that as long as they believe the truth, go to church on Sabbath, and live as good and moral lives as they are able to do, this is all that God expects of us, and that He covers all our discrepancies with the blood and righteousness of Jesus. Unfortunately, those who continue to believe this will wake up too late to make the proper preparations. They will find that they are in the camp of the foolish virgins who have not the extra oil in their lamps. That oil is received in the time of the special heart cleansing spoken of in the previous chapter. As a review, here is a portion of that quotation taken from *The Great Controversy 1888*, p. 425:

> While the investigative Judgment is going forward in Heaven, while the sins of penitent believers are being removed from the sanctuary, there is to be a special work of purification, of putting away of sin, among God's people upon earth.... When this work shall have been accomplished, the followers of Christ will be ready for His appearing.

The condition of God's people after this cleansing experience is described in this quotation:

> Now, while our great High Priest is making the atonement for us, we should seek to become perfect in Christ. Not even by a thought could our Saviour be brought to yield to the power of temptation. Satan finds in human hearts some point where he can gain a foothold; some sinful desire is cherished, by means of which his temptations assert their power. But Christ declared of Himself: 'The prince of this world cometh, and hath nothing in Me.' John 14:30. Satan could find nothing in the Son of God that would enable him to gain

the victory. He had kept His Father's commandments, and there was no sin in Him that Satan could use to his advantage. This is the condition in which those must be found who shall stand in the time of trouble. (*The Great Controversy*, p. 623)

Just think of this challenge! Not one of us can come to this level of perfection unless we have such a constant fellowship and communion with Jesus that His thoughts become ours, His attitudes and feelings about every minute detail of life are transferred from His mind to ours. As Paul has said:

Let this mind be in you, which was also in Christ Jesus. (Phil. 2:5, KJV)

Do not conform to the pattern of this world, but be transformed by the renewing of your mind. Then you will be able to test and approve what God's will is—his good, pleasing and perfect will. (Rom. 12:2)

For who knows a person's thoughts except their own spirit within them? In the same way no one knows the thoughts of God except the Spirit of God. What we have received is not the spirit of the world, but the Spirit who is from God, so that we may understand what God has freely given us…. The person without the Spirit does not accept the things that come from the Spirit of God but considers them foolishness, and cannot understand them because they are discerned only through the Spirit…. But we have the mind of Christ. (1 Cor. 2:11–16)

It is obvious from these texts that Paul's Christianity was an outworking of the Spirit of God in His life. Why, then, did he not reach the state of perfection that is required of those who will live until Jesus comes without seeing death? Paul himself answers this question:

Now it is required that those who have been given a trust must prove faithful. I care very little if I am judged by you or by any human court; indeed, I do not even judge myself. My conscience is clear, but that does not make me innocent. It is the Lord who judges me. Therefore judge nothing before the appointed time; wait until the Lord comes. He will bring to light what is hidden in darkness and will expose the motives of the heart. At that time each will receive their praise from God. (1 Cor. 4:2–5)

Paul here is speaking by inspiration about the future investigative judgment. This becomes clear by his use of the words "the appointed time."

Similar language is used in Daniel's vision of the cleansing of the heavenly sanctuary:

> Then I heard a holy one speaking, and another holy one said to him, 'How long will it take for the vision to be fulfilled—the vision concerning the daily sacrifice, the rebellion that causes desolation, the surrender of the sanctuary and the trampling underfoot of the LORD's people? He said to me, 'It will take 2,300 evenings and mornings; then the sanctuary will be reconsecrated.' While I, Daniel, was watching the vision and trying to understand it, there before me stood one who looked like a man. And I heard a man's voice from the Ulai calling, 'Gabriel, tell this man the meaning of the vision.' As he came near the place where I was standing, I was terrified and fell prostrate. 'Son of man,' he said to me, 'understand that *the vision concerns the time of the end.*' (Dan. 8:13–17, emphasis added).

Paul may not have known the details concerning the investigative judgment as we know it today, for it was then in the far distant future. But since 1844, it has been present truth that all need to know and understand. Our own eternal destiny is at stake! Nothing is more important now than cooperating with Jesus as He wraps up the long, sordid history of the sin problem and prepares a people to represent Him throughout eternity.

> The subject of the sanctuary and the investigative Judgment should be clearly understood by the people of God. All need a knowledge for themselves of the position and work of the great High Priest. Otherwise, it will be impossible for them to exercise the faith which is essential at this time, or to occupy the position which God designs them to fill. (*The Great Controversy 1888*, p. 488)

> There must be a purifying of the soul here upon the earth, in harmony with Christ's cleansing of the sanctuary in heaven. (*Maranatha: The Lord is Coming*, p. 249)

> It is those who by faith follow Jesus in the great work of the atonement who receive the benefits of His mediation in their behalf, while those who reject the light which brings to view this work of ministration are not benefitted thereby. (*The Great Controversy*, p. 430)

This next quote refers to the Great Disappointment in 1844, which is when people first realized the significance of the heavenly sanctuary:

Jesus sent His angels to direct the minds of the disappointed ones to the most holy place, where He had gone to cleanse the sanctuary and make a special atonement for Israel. Jesus told the angels that all who found Him would understand the work which He was to perform. (*Early Writings*, p. 251)

Dear friend, have you found Jesus in the second apartment as He works there to cleanse your life and erase every spot and stain of sin? Do you understand how to cooperate with Him and join Him day by day in the wonderful privilege of getting to know Him in this intimate and loving experience? It is in this way that Jesus prepares His bride to be spotless and ready for the wedding!

The coming of Christ as our high priest to the most holy place, for the cleansing of the sanctuary, brought to view in Daniel 8:14…; the coming of the Lord to His temple, foretold by Malachi, are descriptions of the same event; *and this is also represented by the coming of the bridegroom to the marriage*, described by Christ in the parable of the ten virgins, of Matthew 25. (The Great Controversy, p. 426, emphasis added)

This understanding is vitally important to those who desire to be among the wise virgins. The foolish virgins are not just sleeping while they are waiting for the Bridegroom, they are completely unaware that some of God's people are receiving the extra oil of the latter rain. They are unaware that the cleansing going on in the sanctuary above must also be going on in their lives, in preparation for receiving the seal of God. Too long we have thought that if we are keeping the Sabbath, we have the seal. Just as the Sabbath was the sign of God's finished work of Creation in the beginning, so now the Sabbath will be a sign of the finished work of Jesus' recreation in the life of every believer who will cooperate with Him now. Unfortunately, the foolish virgins will find this out too late to prepare!

When Daniel wanted to look more deeply into these mysteries concerning the end of all things, he was told that this information was not available for him at that time. It was only to be revealed to those who would live at the end of time. That time has now come! But even now, only the wise will understand the refining, purifying process that is absolutely essential:

Many will be purified, made spotless and refined, but the wicked will continue to be wicked. None of the wicked will understand, but those who are wise will understand. (Dan. 12:10)

The book of Daniel is now unsealed, and the revelation made by Christ to John is to come to all the inhabitants of the earth. By the increase of knowledge a people is to be prepared to stand in the latter days. (*Selected Messages*, vol. 2, p. 105)

The Lord leaves in darkness no man who has an ear to hear and a heart to understand. (*The Upward Look*, p. 143)

How I desire to be among the wise, don't you? And we can be! Jesus is longing for everyone to listen to the still, small voice of His Holy Spirit speaking to each heart. Can we turn off the TV and lay aside our busy activities long enough to spend time in His Word and listen to His voice? You will be surprised at the blessed experience that will follow!

Chapter 11

My Own Story

One day when Jesus was busily engaged in healing the sick who had been brought to Him, the Pharisees gathered around as they often did, and began to question Him. "Why do your disciples break the tradition of the elders? They don't wash their hands before they eat!" (Matt. 15:2). In reply, Jesus spoke an amazingly profound statement that is very enlightening for our understanding of the cleansing He is now doing in the Most Holy Place:

> Jesus called the crowd to him and said, 'Listen and understand. What goes into someone's mouth does not defile them, but what comes out of their mouth, that is what defiles them.... Every plant that my heavenly Father has not planted will be pulled up by the roots.... Don't you see that whatever enters the mouth goes into the stomach and then out of the body? But the things that come out of a person's mouth come from the heart, and these defile them. For out of the heart come evil thoughts—murder, adultery, sexual immorality, theft, false testimony, slander. These are what defile a person.' (Matt. 15:10–20)

Another time in a similar discussion with the Pharisees, Jesus said:

'You brood of vipers, how can you who are evil say anything good? For the mouth speaks what the heart is full of. A good man brings good things out of the good stored up in him, and an evil man brings evil things out of the evil stored up in him. But I tell you that everyone will have to give account on the day of judgment for every empty word they have spoken. For by your words you will be acquitted, and by your words you will be condemned.' (Matt. 12:34–37)

This is usually thought of as being true in the process of separating the righteous from the wicked, which takes place at the end of the world. But how many realize that it is also true in the judgment of the living as Jesus separates the evil things out of our lives that Satan has succeeded in placing there? This realization came clear to me in 1974, when I was faced with a challenge in my life that brought out thoughts, feelings, and behaviors that I did not know were in my heart.

It all began when God gave us a precious little son. He was two-and-a-half years old when God led us to him. He was very bright and active, with a cheerful disposition and a happy smile. But he was also hyperactive, and led me for a merry chase! My days were no longer predictable, and my nights were sometimes interrupted, too. In those early months, I found myself feeling resentful, frustrated, and sometimes angry. Often I cried out to God to heal me of these resentful, angry thoughts and feelings that would come when I felt pushed beyond my limit of endurance. I realize now that God was allowing me to experience things that would push me out of my cozy little nest as a well-respected wife, mother, and leader in the church.

As time went by, I continued to feel defeated and angry because of my inability to hold my temper. I had thought I was a good Christian, but now my wrong feelings rose up to mock me. One morning while I was in my worship, I pleaded with God to show me why I could not control the impatient, resentful feelings I would have when I felt pushed beyond my comfort level. Suddenly, I began to see a succession of memory pictures in my mind, all of them about my relationship with my father when I was a child. I saw and felt the frustration and resentment I experienced when my father punished me when I thought it was unfair. I remembered running away to the neighbor's house and telling them how angry I was because of a spanking I had just received from my father. I remembered telling my classmates in school that I hated my father. Remorse overwhelmed me, and I fell weeping onto the bed. Thoughts whirled through my head. What was the meaning of the flashbacks of my childhood experiences with my father? Was God preparing me to die?

Finally, I collected my thoughts enough to pray. "Lord, why are you showing me all these scenes from my childhood? And why are they all about my relationship with my father?" The answer I felt God gave me surprised me. I came to understand that God desired me to go to my father and confess of my rebellious and hateful spirit toward him. I was shocked! I had always felt that my feelings were legitimate and that my father was at fault for his treatment of me. When I expressed this to the Lord, His Spirit reminded me that my father is responsible to Him for how he treated me, and I am responsible to Him for how I responded to my father. So, as soon as I could make the trip to my parents' home, I went to my father and confessed that God had revealed to me that I had been rebellious and angry toward him when I was a child, and I asked his forgiveness. For the first time that I could remember, he threw his arms around me and said, "Carol, I have been thinking that I should come back to God. Please pray for me!" That was the beginning of his journey, and years later, after living in my home for eight years, he fell asleep in Jesus at the age of 85.

Not long after this, again while I was in prayer, I had another series of flashbacks on a different subject in my childhood, and then later another. I asked several ministers what they thought this strange experience could mean, but no one had an answer for me. Then one morning while I was again in worship, I began having flashbacks of all romantic emotions and daydreams I had ever experienced about boys in my life, and then men as I grew older, right up to that present moment. I felt devastated and frightened! What could be the purpose of all of this? I began to be afraid, and then angry, especially when it came to my mind that this might be the work of Satan, the accuser of God's people. I already had confessed and put away the inappropriate thoughts I had about men, and I was not even praying about that subject when the flashbacks began.

Rising from my worship chair, I went into the kitchen and began washing the supper dishes that had been left in the sink from the night before. "What is going on in my life?" I cried out to God. "I have to know if this is Satan trying to trick me. It isn't like You to take me through something I don't understand. If this is You, please tell me why You are taking me through this!" After a moment, I found myself impressed to look up the final atonement. I knew from my former studies that this would be found in the writings of Ellen White concerning the work of Christ in the heavenly sanctuary. Drying my hands, I went quickly to the library and took out *The Great Controversy*. Opening the book, I began to read:

> The judgment is now passing in the sanctuary above. For many years this work has been in progress. Soon—none know how soon—it will pass to the cases of the living. In the awful presence of God our lives are to come up in review. (p. 490)

I felt a calm presence and an overwhelming sensation that this was happening to me. I was stunned! "I thought that we would not know when our names come up in the judgment until after the close of probation," I said with growing excitement. I felt encouraged to keep reading, so I did.

> At this time above all others it behooves every soul to heed the Saviour's admonition: 'Watch and pray: for ye know not when the time is.' ... 'If therefore thou shalt not watch, I will come on thee as a thief, and thou shalt not know what hour I will come upon thee' (Ibid.)

God impressed upon me that because I had been watching and praying, I was able to participate with Jesus as He went through my books to cleanse them. As the significance of this penetrated into my mind, I felt a holy joy and excitement I had never before experienced. The judgment of the living had begun, and it was not secret! No more fear of coming to the close of probation and learning too late that I was lost! I could hardly believe it. I wanted to shout it from the rooftop to all of my fellow Adventist believers, "Jesus will walk with you through the judgment! You don't have to be afraid anymore."

Needless to say, my life has never been the same again. I began studying the sanctuary and learning more about the experiential meaning of each part of the sanctuary service. I shared in a limited way until God opened the door for me to travel and speak around the world through my association with American Christian Ministries. And now, time is running out. Only a few years remain before Jesus closes His work in the heavenly sanctuary. It is my purpose in writing this book to share with everyone who will read these pages that Jesus is still waiting for you to join Him in the final stages before His intercession ceases and the door to the second apartment closes. He loves you, dear Reader. Please join Him now! He waits with arms outstretched for you to come while there is still time to be healed, time to be ready when He comes to bring us home.

Chapter 12

The Abyss

As I said in the prologue, I have written this book as a follow-up of my book entitled, *Countdown! 7 Trumpets for Today*, in which I described the present application of the seven trumpets of Revelation 8 and 9. Briefly, these are:

#1. The fall of the towers in New York City, September 11, 2001.

#2. Natural disasters such as the great tsunami of December 25, 2004; Hurricanes Katrina and Rita in the spring of 2005.

#3. Fall of the economy on September 14, 15 of 2008.

#4. Three and one-half years of Papal rise to power and emphasis of the importance of Sunday, beginning with Pope Benedict's Family Day in May/June of 2012, and culminating with the visit of Pope Francis to America on September 22-26, 2015.

#5. First woe: demons let out of the abyss; Muslim hoards come out of their land to attack people in other parts of the world.

#6. Second woe: escalating war with Islam; close of probation; seven last plagues; Armageddon.

#7. Third woe: the coming of Christ.

As you can see, we are just now in the beginning of the first woe. In order to understand the seriousness of this time for everyone living on planet earth, I want to dissect the meaning of the scriptural clues, which are present in the fifth trumpet. First, the meaning of the word, "woe," is significant. Throughout Scripture, woes are pronounced upon a generation of people whose probationary time is ending. Here are several examples:

In Matthew 23:13–29, Jesus pronounces seven woes on the teachers of the law and the Pharisees. Then He says:

> Go ahead, then, and complete what your ancestors started! You snakes! You brood of vipers! How will you escape being condemned to hell…? And so upon you will come all the righteous blood that has been shed on earth…. Truly I tell you, all this will come on this generation. Jerusalem, Jerusalem, you who kill the prophets and stone those sent to you, how often I have longed to gather your children together, as a hen gathers her chicks under her wings, and you were not willing. Look, your house is left to you desolate. (Matt. 23:32–38)

In Isaiah 5:8–22, six woes are pronounced upon God's people of that generation. Here God gives the reason why He is abandoning His people to destruction:

> What more could have been done for my vineyard than I have done for it? When I looked for good grapes, why did it yield only bad? Now I will tell you what I am going to do to my vineyard: I will take away its hedge, and it will be destroyed; I will break down its wall, and it will be trampled. I will make it a wasteland, neither pruned nor cultivated, and briers and thorns will grow there…. For they have rejected the law of the LORD Almighty and spurned the word of the Holy One of Israel. Therefore the LORD's anger burns against his people; his hand is raised and he strikes them down. (Isa. 5:4–6, 24, 25)

For three sins of Judah, even for four, I will not relent. Because they have rejected the law of the LORD and have not kept his decrees, because they have been led astray by false gods, the gods their ancestors followed, I will send fire upon Judah that will consume the fortresses of Jerusalem. (Amos 2:4, 5)

Put the trumpet to your lips! An eagle is over the house of the LORD because the people have broken my covenant and rebelled against my law. Israel cries out to me, 'Our God, we acknowledge you!' But Israel has rejected what is good...; They offer sacrifices as gifts to me, and ... the LORD is not pleased with them. Now he will remember their wickedness and punish their sins. (Hos. 8:1–3, 13, emphasis added)

Notice the consistency of these Scriptures. They point out that the breaking of God's law, regardless of the profession of faith, brings disaster. The whole Bible is consistent on this matter. So it will be for the final generation of earth's history. We have now come to this crisis—the crisis of the ages—the final countdown to the coming of Jesus. Please notice the description of the woes that are facing us at this time when the fifth trumpet is beginning to sound: "As I watched, I heard an eagle that was flying in midair call out in a loud voice: 'Woe! Woe! Woe to the inhabitants of the earth, because of the trumpet blasts about to be sounded by the other three angels!'" (Rev. 8:13).

Trumpets in the Bible were sounded as an alarm of war or coming invasion or disaster. The symbol of an eagle would likely represent "the rapid, dread swoop of an eagle upon its prey" (*The Seventh-day Adventist Commentary*, vol. 4, p. 910), or an omen of doom (Ibid., vol. 7, p. 789).

The fifth angel sounded his trumpet, and I saw a star that had fallen from the sky to the earth. The star was given the key to the shaft of the Abyss. When he opened the Abyss, smoke rose from it like the smoke from a gigantic furnace. The sun and sky were darkened by the smoke from the Abyss. And out of the smoke locusts came down on the earth and were given power like that of scorpions of the earth. They were told not to harm the grass of the earth or any plant or tree, *but only those people who did not have the seal of God on their foreheads*.... During those days men will seek death but will not find it; they will long to die, but death will elude them. (Rev. 9:1–6, emphasis added)

The seriousness of this trumpet—the beginning of the three-point countdown ending in the coming of Jesus—cannot be overestimated. There is a sudden change in the spiritual and social climate of earth that affects everyone on the planet. A clearer understanding of this trumpet can be seen in Ezekiel's vision of the withdrawal of the glory of the presence of God from the temple as recorded in Ezekiel, chapters 8–11. Because of the wickedness of the spiritual leaders of Israel, God warned them that He would be forced to withdraw from them. The crowning insult to His holy presence was sun worship:

> He then brought me into the inner court of the house of the LORD, and there at the entrance to the temple ... were about twenty-five men. With their backs toward the temple of the LORD and their faces toward the east, they were bowing down to the sun in the east. (Ezek. 8:16)

Reluctantly, the glory of the Lord moved from the cherubim to the threshold (see Ezek. 9:3), stopped briefly at the east gate (see Ezek. 10:19), then "went up from within the city and stopped above the mountain east of it" (Ezek. 11:23). In the meantime, judgments were being poured out upon the city.

> Then I heard him call out in a loud voice, 'Bring near those who are appointed to execute judgment in the city, each with a weapon in his hand.... Go throughout the city of Jerusalem and put a mark on the foreheads of those who grieve and lament over all the detestable things that are done in it.... Slaughter the old men, the young men and women, the mothers and children, but do not touch anyone who has the mark. Begin at my sanctuary.' So they began with the old men who were in front of the temple. (Ezek. 9:1–6)

Who were the elders who were slain first? No doubt they were the same ones who, with their backs toward the temple and their faces toward the east, were bowing down to the sun. This is what brought about the fall of Jerusalem and the beginning of God's judgments upon the nation of Israel. Only those who had the mark of God upon their foreheads were spared. Is not this a perfect parallel to the movement for Sunday worship that is happening today? Led by the two recent popes, the emphasis for the importance of worship on Sunday is being urged. And what is to follow for our land—yes, even for the world—if this universal day of worship becomes law? The answer is in the Scriptures:

> I will not look on them with pity or spare them. Although they shout in my ears, I will not listen to them. (Ezek. 8:18)

I will execute judgment on you…. And you will know that I am the LORD, for you have not followed my decrees or kept my laws but have conformed to the standards of the nations around you. (Ezek. 11:11, 12)

Ellen White also comments on Ezekiel's vision and applies it to the end of time:

The mark of deliverance has been set upon those 'that sigh and that cry for all the abominations that be done.' Now the angel of death goes forth, represented in Ezekiel's vision by the men with the slaughtering weapons…. *The work of destruction begins among those who have professed to be the guardians of the people. The false watchmen are the first to fall.* (The Great Controversy, p. 656, emphasis added)

The angel is to place a mark upon the forehead of all who are separated from sin and sinners, and the destroying angel will follow, to slay utterly both old and young. (*Testimonies for the Church*, vol. 5, p. 505)

Now, let's return to the fifth trumpet and study more deeply into the meaning. The star that has fallen to the earth symbolizes Satan (see *The Seventh-day Adventist Bible Commentary*, vol. 7, p. 791). When he is given the key to the Abyss, he now has God's permission to allow the hosts of darkness to escape the restrictions that have been placed upon them and come out into the world with all their evil intentions. What implication does this have for the inhabitants of the earth? To understand this better, it is important to have a clearer concept of the abyss. It is not some subterranean cavern or yawning chasm somewhere in the universe. It is merely a symbolic way of showing how Satan's activities are brought to a halt (Ibid., p. 878). This fact is made clear in Revelation 20:1–3:

And I saw an angel coming down out of heaven, having the key to the Abyss and holding in his hand a great chain. He seized the dragon, that ancient serpent, who is the devil, or Satan, and bound him for a thousand years. *He threw him into the Abyss, and locked and sealed it over him, to keep him from deceiving the nations* anymore until the thousand years were ended. After that, he must be set free for a short time. (emphasis added)

Although this passage is speaking specifically about the desolation of the earth after Jesus comes and takes His faithful people to heaven, it still identifies the abyss as a place and/or condition where Satan is *restricted from tempting anyone*.

Another clue to the abyss is found in Luke 8:26–33. There we see a demon-possessed man who had been driven into solitary places by the demon controlling him. When Jesus was about to drive the demon out of the man, the demon begged not to be sent to the abyss, but to be sent into a herd of pigs feeding on a hillside nearby. Jesus obliged, and the pigs rushed down the bank and were drowned in the lake. Perhaps Jesus permitted this to happen to demonstrate that even animals are tortured and unhappy when demons inhabit them!

In Matthew 12:43–45, Jesus told a story that further illustrates some of the behavioral patterns of demons:

> *When an impure spirit comes out of a person, it goes through arid places seeking rest and does not find it.* Then it says, 'I will return to the house I left.' When it arrives, it finds the house unoccupied, swept clean and put in order. Then it goes and takes with it seven other spirits more wicked than itself, and they go in and live there. And the final condition of that person is worse than the first. That is how it will be with this wicked generation. (emphasis added)

From these few clues, we can conclude that when demons are cast out, they are sent by God to arid or waste places where their opportunities to tempt people are curtailed. Therefore, when the shaft to the Abyss is opened, much more spiritual darkness and demonic activity are to be expected.

> We are living in the time of the end. The fast-fulfilling signs of the times declare that the coming of Christ is near at hand…. The Spirit of God is gradually but surely being withdrawn from the earth. Plagues and judgments are already falling upon the despisers of the grace of God. The calamities by land and sea, the unsettled state of society, the alarms of war, are portentous. They forecast approaching events of the greatest magnitude. The agencies of evil are combining their forces and consolidating. They are strengthening for the last great crisis. Great changes are soon to take place in our world, and the final movements will be rapid ones. The condition of things in our world shows that troublous times are right upon us. (*Testimonies for the Church*, vol. 9, p. 11)

I was shown that the time was in the near future that those whom God had warned and reproved and given great light but they would not correct their ways and follow the light, He would remove from them that heavenly protection which had preserved them from Satan's cruel power; the Lord would surely leave them to themselves to follow the judgment and counsels of their own wisdom; they would be simply left to themselves, and the protection of God be withdrawn from them, and they would not be shielded from the working of Satan. (*Manuscript Release 14*, p. 2)

We can now more clearly see that it is of utmost importance to understand the meaning and purpose of the seal of God and how to receive it. This will be the subject of our next and final chapter.

Chapter 13

Receiving the Seal

The heavenly hosts have long awaited the time when the great controversy will be finished and sin and sinners will be no more. Patiently they have labored for the Father and the Son, working side by side with Jesus to win as many as possible to accept the plan of salvation. Now, as the end draws near, all heaven is astir with activity.

> It is impossible to give any idea of the experience of the people of God who shall be alive upon the earth when celestial glory and a repetition of the persecutions of the past are blended. They will walk in the light proceeding from the throne of God. By means of the angels there will be constant communication between heaven and earth. (*Testimonies for the Church,* vol. 9, p. 16)

It is almost time to place the mark of God's approval upon the foreheads of those who have accepted God's call and have proved faithful during the worldwide apostasy at the end of time (Rev. 17:1–14). But wait! A mighty angel from heaven flies swiftly from heaven to earth with an urgent message to give to the four angels, who are stationed at the four corners of the earth. The scene is recorded in Revelation 7:1–4:

> After this I saw four angels standing at the four corners of the earth, holding back the four winds of the earth to prevent any wind from blowing on the land or on the sea or on any tree. Then I saw another angel coming up from the east, having the seal of the living God. He called out in a loud voice to the four angels who had been given power to harm the land and the sea: *'Do not harm the land or the sea or the trees until we put a seal on the foreheads of the servants of our God.'* Then I heard the number of those who were sealed: 144,000 from all the tribes of Israel. (emphasis added)

This delay has been in progress for a number of years. God has given His people ample time to do the work of personal preparation, as well as sharing with others the message of His soon return. But this additional time is rapidly coming to a close. The message in the fifth trumpet is a warning that God is beginning to let the winds go and that every person on earth will soon have chosen their final destiny.

> Time is very short, and all that is to be done must be done quickly. The angels are holding the four winds, and Satan is taking advantage of everyone who is not fully established in the truth. Every soul is to be tested. *Every defect in the character, unless it is overcome by the help of God's Spirit, will become a sure means of destruction.* I feel as never before the necessity for our people to be energized by the spirit of the truth, for Satan's devices will ensnare every soul who has not made God his strength. (*Testimonies for the Church*, vol. 5, p. 573, emphasis supplied)

> Already kingdom is rising against kingdom. There is not now a determined engagement. As yet *the four winds are held until the servants of God shall be sealed in their foreheads.* Then the powers of earth will marshal their forces for the last great battle. How carefully we should improve the little remaining period of our probation! (*The Seventh-day Adventist Bible Commentary*, vol. 7, p. 968, emphasis added)

For review, let's consider again the message, which contains the fifth trumpet:

> The fifth angel sounded his trumpet, and I saw a star that had fallen from the sky to the earth. The star was given the key to the shaft of the Abyss. When he opened the Abyss, smoke rose from it like the smoke from a gigantic furnace. The sun and sky were darkened by the smoke from the Abyss. And out of the smoke locusts came down on the earth and were given power like that of scorpions of the earth. They were told not to harm the grass of the earth or any plant or tree, *but only those people who did not have the seal of God on their foreheads*.... During those days people will seek death but will not find it; they will long to die, but death will elude them. (Rev. 9:1–6, emphasis added)

The most important part of the message of the fifth trumpet is that God has made a way of escape for all who will avail themselves of this provision. Just as God provided an ark of safety when He sent the flood upon the earth, so now He is inviting all who will heed His trumpet warnings to come into the safety provided by His seal. What a wonderful God we have, who refuses to allow His chosen ones to be at the mercy of the wrath of the demons. Even the very word "seal" is descriptive of God's loving care.

In Greek, the word "sphragizo" means to seal, put a mark on an object to show possession, authority, identity, or security. God wants His people to be so committed to Him that He can put His seal of ownership upon them; thus, they will be impregnable to the assaults of Satan, both within and without. Jesus said of Himself:

> The prince of this world is coming. He has no hold over me, but he comes so that the world may learn that I love the Father and do exactly what my Father has commanded me. (John 14:30, 31)

> I do nothing on my own but speak just what the Father has taught me. The one who sent me is with me; he has not left me alone, for I always do what pleases him. (John 8:28, 29)

> Do not work for food that spoils, but for food that endures to eternal life, which the Son of Man will give you. *For on him God the Father has placed his seal of approval.* (John 6:27, emphasis supplied)

Jesus is our example, showing us how to be prepared to receive the seal of God's approval, and thus be protected from the assaults of Satan. Just as Jesus said on the eve of His betrayal, "The prince of this world is coming," so we also are on the eve of the time of trouble when Satan will be permitted to unleash the powers of darkness in ways that have never been seen in the world until now. We must have the seal of God's approval and ownership to escape the trials and torments that God will permit to happen to the inhabitants of earth before He comes. The key is found in the life of Jesus, who did nothing on His own, but only what He received from continual communication with His Father.

> Angels of God will preserve His people while they walk in the path of duty, but there is no assurance of such protection for those who deliberately venture upon Satan's ground.... Could the veil be lifted, we would see evil angels pressing their darkness around us and working with all their power to deceive and destroy. Wicked men are surrounded, influenced, and aided by evil spirits. The man of faith and prayer has yielded his soul to divine guidance, and angels of God bring to him light and strength from heaven. (*Testimonies for the Church*, vol. 5, pp. 198, 199)

> Not even by a thought could our Saviour be brought to yield to the power of temptation. This is the condition in which those must be found who shall stand in the time of trouble. (*The Great Controversy*, p. 623)

Please do not become discouraged when you read this! God has provided a way for every person to be cleansed and prepared if they will. No one can cleanse himself of sin's defilement. It is only possible through a constant relationship with Jesus.

> The Lord would have all His sons and daughters happy, peaceful, and obedient.... Through faith, every deficiency of character may be supplied, every defilement cleansed, every fault corrected, every excellence developed. (*From Trials to Triumph*, p. 296)

> The Lord is looking upon men in the different spheres in which they move, and the character is tested under the different circumstances in which they are placed. (*The Seventh-day Adventist Bible Commentary*, vol. 4, p. 1181)

> As fire purifies gold, so Christ purifies His people by temptation and trial. (*This Day With God*, p. 259)

> Everything in our character that cannot enter the city of God will be reproved; if we submit to the Lord's refining, all the dross and tin will be consumed. (*The Seventh-day Adventist Bible Commentary*, vol. 4, p. 1181)

Are we striving with all our God-given powers to reach the measure of the stature of men and women in Christ? Are we seeking for his fullness, ever reaching higher and higher, trying to attain to the perfection of his character? When God's servants reach this point, they will be sealed in their foreheads. The recording angel will declare, 'It is done.' They will be complete in Him whose they are by creation and redemption. (*Selected Messages*, vol. 3, p. 427)

How can anyone come to such a state of perfection? First, it is important to understand the meaning of the word "character." "The thoughts and feelings combined make up the moral character" (*Testimonies for the Church*, vol. 5, p. 310). All our thoughts and feelings must be in agreement with God's thoughts and feelings about everything in our lives. As Paul says in 2 Corinthians 10:5, "We take captive *every thought* to make it obedient to Christ" (emphasis added).

Wrong dispositions and feelings are to be rooted out. (*The Upward Look*, p. 218)

Few realize that it is a duty to exercise control over the thoughts and imaginations.... When the mind is not under the direct influence of the Spirit of God, Satan can mold it as he chooses. (*In Heavenly Places*, p. 163)

There is not an impulse of our nature ... or an inclination of the heart, but needs to be, moment by moment, under the control of the Spirit of God.... [We] should ever walk humbly before the Lord, pleading in faith that God will direct every thought and control every impulse. (*Patriarchs and Prophets*, p. 421)

If Christ is abiding in the heart, He will be in all our thoughts.... Those who have trained the mind to delight in spiritual exercises are the ones who can be translated and not be overwhelmed with the purity and transcendent glory of heaven. (In Heavenly Places, p. 163)

For me, this would be impossible without a practical, working understanding of the sanctuary. The various steps in the sanctuary illustrate the components of thought that must regulate all our thinking and feeling. Thus, it is a type of check list that reminds us constantly what thoughts and feelings are in harmony with the mind and heart of God. In review, these steps are:

1. Praise, thanksgiving, trust in God.

2. Repentance, humility, being patient, and forgiving toward others.

3. Apply Scripture to every experience and life situation; claim the promises that apply to your need.

4. Fruit of the Spirit: love, joy, peace, longsuffering, gentleness, goodness, faith, meekness, temperance.

5. Focusing on the life of Jesus and maintaining a constant connection with Him.

6. Interceding for self and others.

7. Submitting to Jesus' cleansing work in every aspect of our life, from conception until the present.

Daily, moment by moment, I keep my mind in the sanctuary with Jesus. He guides, comforts, corrects, instructs, and protects me from the thoughts and feelings that the devil wants to place in my mind. If I succumb to the evil one, even in the slightest degree, I turn quickly to Jesus, and He forgives and cleanses me. There is no hope without this constant communion with Jesus.

> Now it is God who makes both us and you stand firm in Christ. He anointed us, set his seal of ownership on us, and put his Spirit in our hearts as a deposit, guaranteeing what is to come. (2 Cor. 1:21, 22)

> And you also were included in Christ when you heard the word of truth, the gospel of your salvation. When you believed, you were marked in him with a seal, the promised Holy Spirit, who is a deposit guaranteeing our inheritance until the redemption of those who are God's possession—to the praise of his glory. (Eph. 1:13, 14)

> Consider therefore the kindness and sternness of God: sternness to those who fell, but kindness to you, provided that you continue in his kindness. Otherwise, you also will be cut off. (Rom. 11:22)

Notice that Paul says in these texts that when we accept Jesus as our Savior, we are given the seal of the Holy Spirit as a deposit that guarantees our eternal inheritance, *as long as we continue to have a personal relationship with Him.* This has been the case since the beginning of time until now. But for the final generation, there must be a finished work of redemption. Probation is about to close, and the people of God must now go through the special work of cleansing, which will seal them in forever. This experience is not easy, and many people will not endure to the end. But for those who do, the seal of God will protect them through the time of trouble and keep them in the ark of safety until He comes.

> I was shown the startling fact that but a small portion of those who now profess the truth will be sanctified by it and be saved. Many will get above the simplicity of the work. They will conform to the world, cherish idols, and become spiritually dead. The humble, self-sacrificing followers of Jesus will pass on to perfection, leaving behind the indifferent and lovers of the world. (*Testimonies for the Church*, vol. 1, pp. 608, 609)

> I saw a covering that God was drawing over His people to protect them in the time of trouble; and every soul that was decided on the truth and was pure in heart was to be covered with the covering of the Almighty. (*Early Writings*, p. 43)

> I saw that many were neglecting the preparation so needful and were looking to the time of 'refreshing' and the 'latter rain' to fit them to stand in the day of the Lord and to live in His sight. Oh, how many I saw in the time of trouble without a shelter! They had neglected the needful preparation; therefore they could not receive the refreshing that all must have to fit them to live in the sight of a holy God. (Ibid., p. 71)

> As mercy's sweet voice died away, fear and horror seized the wicked.... Those who had not prized God's word were hurrying to and fro, wandering from sea to sea, and from north to the east, to seek the Word of the Lord.... What would they not give for one word of approval from God! (Ibid., p. 281)

What is this "needful preparation" that all must have to receive the final seal of God? I am going to use excerpts from *Early Writings* to vividly describe this experience:

> I saw some, with strong faith and agonizing cries, pleading with God.... Now and then their faces would light up with the marks of God's approbation, and again the same solemn, earnest, anxious look would settle upon them. Evil angels crowded around, pressing darkness upon them to shut out Jesus from their view, that their eyes

might be drawn to the darkness that surrounded them.... Their only safety was in keeping their eyes directed upward. Angels of God ... were continually wafting their wings over them to scatter the thick darkness. As the praying ones continued their earnest cries, at times a ray of light from Jesus came to them, to encourage their hearts and light up their countenances. Some, I saw, did not participate in this work of agonizing and pleading. They seemed indifferent and careless. They were not resisting the darkness around them, and it shut them in like a thick cloud. The angels of God left these and went to the aid of the earnest, praying ones.... Soon I heard a voice like many musical instruments all sounding in perfect strains, sweet and harmonious. It surpassed any music I had ever heard, seeming to be full of mercy, compassion, and elevating, holy joy.... My attention was then turned to the company I had seen, who were mightily shaken.... The company of guardian angels around them had been doubled, and they were clothed with an armor from their head to their feet. They moved in exact order, like a company of soldiers.... Their features ... now shone with the light and glory of heaven. They had obtained the victory, and it called forth from them the deepest gratitude and holy, sacred joy. The numbers of the company had lessened.... The careless and indifferent, who did not join with those who prized victory and salvation to perseveringly plead and agonize for it, did not obtain it, and they were left behind in darkness, and their places were immediately filled by others taking hold of the truth.... *Evil angels still pressed around them, but could have no power over them*.... I asked what had made this great change. An angel answered, 'It is the latter rain, the refreshing from the presence of the Lord, the loud cry of the third angel.' (pp. 269–271, emphasis added)

As you read this description of God's faithful people, do you catch the thrill of being an overcomer? Can you just imagine what it would feel like to be impervious to the temptations and power of the evil one? This is the experience of those who go through the cleansing of Jesus in the second apartment of the sanctuary. It is called the Most Holy Place because it is through this experience that brings God's people into complete and perfect harmony with Him in everything. Satan has no more access to them because everything that Satan has planted in their hearts throughout their lives has been revealed to them by Jesus, and has been purged and rooted out and replaced with the mind of Christ—His thoughts and feelings, His love for people, His willingness to suffer for the salvation of others, His perfect union with His Father. Thus, the fullness of the Holy Spirit can be poured out without measure into their hearts. The seal of God is placed upon their foreheads because their minds are in complete harmony with God the Father and the Son.

> Then I looked, and there before me was the Lamb, standing on Mount Zion, and with him 144,000, who had his name and his Father's name written on their foreheads.... They follow the Lamb wherever he goes. They were purchased from among mankind and offered as firstfruits to God and the Lamb. No lie was found in their mouths; they are blameless. (Rev. 14:1, 4, 5)

Dear friend, are you willing to go through the effort that it takes to cooperate with Jesus as He gently invites you to come into the cleansing experience with Him? Are you willing to let go of everything in your life that would prevent you from coming into complete and total harmony with His mind in every area of your life? If you do, you can be assured that Satan and his evil hosts will oppose you. They will try to bring darkness into your mind, overwhelm you with guilt, and bring people into your life to attack you, criticize you, and tempt you to sin. They will use your faults and failings to discourage you, and they will tell you that you are already lost and hopeless. They will try in every way possible to separate you from Jesus.

Fortunately, Jesus has provided for us the sanctuary to which we can run for safety! Through the principles found there, we can keep our minds looking upward. We can keep cheerful, hopeful, and praise God all the time. We can empty our minds of sin and guilt at the cross. We can claim the words of Scripture as our source of comfort, strength, and hope. We can be filled by the Spirit and communicate with Jesus every moment. We can be surrounded and protected by the mighty angels who continually minister to us and keep the evil one at bay.

> As the vine branch constantly draws the sap from the living vine, so are we to cling to Jesus, and receive from Him by faith the strength and perfection of His own character. (*The Desire of Ages*, p. 676)

> The seal of the living God will be placed upon those only who bear a likeness to Christ in character. As wax takes the impression of the seal, so the soul is to take the impression of the Spirit of God and retain the image of Christ. (*The Seventh-day Adventist Bible Commentary*, vol. 7, p. 970)

Just think of it! The closer we are to Jesus, the more we cling to Him and communicate with Him, the more we assimilate His thoughts and feelings about everything. Don't fool yourself into believing that you can have a little of the world and a little of Jesus and still be a victorious Christian. That is like drinking a glass of juice that is laced with poison. You cannot have a mixture of good and evil and be prepared to live eternally with Jesus.

> Do not be yoked together with unbelievers. For what do righteousness and wickedness have in common? Or what fellowship can light have with darkness? What harmony is there between Christ and Belial? Or what does a believer have in common with an unbeliever? What agreement is there between the temple of God and idols? For we are the temple of the living God. As God has said: 'I will live with them and walk among them, and I will be their God, and they will be my people.' Therefore, 'Come out from them and be separate, says the Lord. Touch no unclean thing, and I will receive you.' And, 'I will be a Father to you, and you will be my sons and daughters, says the Lord Almighty.' Therefore, since we have these promises, dear friends, let us purify ourselves from everything that contaminates body and spirit, perfecting holiness out of reverence for God. (2 Cor. 6:14–7:1)

Notice that Paul says that we are the temple of the living God! That is why the sanctuary is the pattern for our perfection of character. God designed the sanctuary to contain all the elements of His character, which will bring us into perfect harmony with His mind. Therefore, we will be measured in the judgment by these principles.

> The sins of Israel must go to judgment beforehand. Every sin must be confessed at the sanctuary, *then the work will move*, it must be done *now*. The latter rain is coming on those that are pure—all, then, will receive it as formerly. None receive the latter rain but those who do all they can. (Elder A. T. Jones, "The Third Angel's Message," *General Conference Daily Bulletin*, vol. 5, 1893)

> The Heart-searcher ... is weighing moral character in the golden scales of the heavenly sanctuary. (*Sons and Daughters of God*, p. 60)

> We individually have a case pending in the court of heaven. *Character is being weighed in the balances of the sanctuary* and it should be the earnest desire of all to walk humbly and carefully, lest ... they fail of the grace of God and lose everything that is valuable. All

dissension, all differences and faultfinding, should be put away, with all evil speaking and bitterness; kindness, love, and compassion for one another should be cherished, that the prayer of Christ that His disciples might be one as He is with the Father may be answered. (*Testimonies for the Church*, vol. 5, p. 279, emphasis added)

Dear friend, as you read these pages, the events of the fifth trumpet have already begun. God is withdrawing His Spirit from the earth and allowing its inhabitants to have the leader they have chosen. The devil and his army of evil angels are being let loose to bring more havoc into society than we ever seen before. "The Lord is removing His restrictions from the earth.... Those who are without God's protection will find no safety in any place or position" (*Testimonies for the Church*, vol. 8, p. 50).

But God's people will be safe from their attacks! Surrounded and protected by holy angels, they will go forth to preach the last warning message to the world. Through the time of trouble such as never was, they will be protected from starvation and death. They will behold the reward of the wicked who are slain by the brightness of Jesus' coming. And then they will receive the reward of the righteous as He comes to receive His own! May we all be faithful until that glorious day, which is so soon to come!

> For the Lord himself will come down from heaven, with a loud command, with the voice of the archangel and with the trumpet call of God, and the dead in Christ will rise first. After that, we who are still alive and are left will be caught up together with them in the clouds to meet the Lord in the air. And so we will be with the Lord forever. Therefore encourage one another with these words. (1 Thess. 4:16–18)

Addendum

Power over Demons

Since the papal visit on September 22–26, 2015, many of us have sensed a shift in the mental and emotional atmosphere. On September 27, in my morning worship, I felt the Lord ask me to set aside one extra day a month to fast and pray for my children. Since I already fast every Friday until Sabbath lunch, I added a partial fast on Thursday of just fruit and some peanuts for strength. On Sabbath morning, October 3, I awakened at 2:30 a.m. I immediately got up, and for three and a half hours I prayed for myself and my children. While I was praying, I could sense evil angels crowding around, whispering dark messages to me, but I prayed until they were gone. I haven't sensed them again, but I am careful to keep my thoughts constantly in tune with the Holy Spirit and Jesus at all times!

Since then I have been amazed that nearly every person that I have been counseling has called me in tears, sometimes in an agony of spirit because of darkness, oppression, accusing voices, terrifying dreams, or mental visions. I explain to each one that we have now begun the fifth trumpet, and the demons are allowed to have more access to us unless we are in the sanctuary with Jesus in our minds and thoughts. Each person has come out of these experiences with a greater understanding of the battle. They have greater faith and determination to triumph over the darkness and to walk continually in the light with Jesus.

For those of you who are reading this book, I am including some Scriptures and Spirit of Prophecy quotations that I hope will be helpful to you. Remember that there are generational demons that have come down through families, and now have more access to harass you and your dear ones if you do not watch and pray. This is why prayers in the Bible often included the sins of the person's ancestors.

> I, the LORD your God, am a jealous God, punishing the children for the sin of the parents to the third and fourth generation of those who hate me, but showing love to a thousand generations of those who love me and keep my commandments. (Deut. 5:9, 10)

> Those of you who are left will waste away in the lands of their enemies because of their sins; also because of their ancestors' sins they will waste away. But if they will confess their sins and the sins of their ancestors ... I will remember my covenant with Jacob and my covenant with Isaac and my covenant with Abraham, and I will remember the land. (Lev. 26:39–42)

> It is inevitable that children should suffer from the consequences of parental wrongdoing, but they are not punished for the parents' guilt, except as they participate in their sins. It is usually the case, however, that children walk in the steps of their parents. By inheritance and example the sons become partakers of the father's sin. Wrong tendencies, perverted appetites, and debased morals, as well as physical disease and degeneracy, are transmitted as a legacy from father to son, to the third and fourth generation. (*Patriarchs and Prophets*, p. 306)

> The habits formed in youth, although they may in after-life be somewhat modified, are seldom essentially changed. Your entire life has been molded by the legacy of character transmitted to you at birth. Your father's perverse temperament is seen in his children. (*Testimonies for the Church*, vol. 4, p. 499)

By heredity and cultivation, the sins and the demons who are attached to these sins are passed on to every person. This is why the special cleansing during the judgment of the living includes our relationship with our forefathers and our family members. They are a part of who we are! This is the experience that is missing in the foolish virgins.

> The class represented by the foolish virgins ... have not ... permitted their old nature to be broken up.... The foolish virgins have been content with a superficial work. They do not know God. They have not studied His character; they have not held communion with Him; therefore they do not know how to trust, how to look and live. Their service to God degenerates into a form. (*Christ's Object Lessons*, p. 411)

> While pride, variance, and strife for supremacy are cherished, the heart cannot enter into fellowship with Christ. (*The Desire of Ages*, p. 650)

> If they cherish hereditary and cultivated traits of character that misrepresent Christ, while professedly His disciples, they are represented by the ... foolish virgins. (*The Seventh-day Adventist Bible Commentary*, vol. 4, p. 1179)

> Inherited and cultivated tendencies to wrong must be crucified. (*Messages to Young People*, p. 68)

The only way to battle against the demonic forces is through fervent prayer. For parents of young children, you can do this in prayer for them:

> Children who have not experienced the cleansing power of Jesus are the lawful prey of the enemy, and the evil angels have easy access to them. Some parents are careless and suffer their children to grow up with but little restraint. Parents have a great work to do in this matter by correcting and training their children, and in bringing them to God and claiming His blessing upon them. By the faithful and untiring efforts of the parents, and the blessing of grace bestowed upon the children in response to the prayers of the parents, the power of the evil angels may be broken and a sanctifying influence shed upon the children. Thus the powers of darkness will be driven back. (*Counsels to Parents, Teachers, and Students*, p. 118)

> Whoever fears the LORD has a secure fortress, and for their children it will be a refuge. (Prov. 14:26.)

> But this is what the LORD says: 'Yes, captives will be taken from warriors, and plunder retrieved from the fierce; I will contend with

those who contend with you, and your children I will save.' (Isa. 49:25)

Battle help for everyone:

I saw evil angels contending for souls, and angels of God resisting them. The conflict was severe. Evil angels were crowding about them, corrupting the atmosphere with their poisonous influence, and stupefying their sensibilities. Holy angels were anxiously watching these souls, and were waiting to drive back Satan's host. But it is not the work of good angels to control minds against the will of the individuals. If they yield to the enemy, and make no effort to resist him, then the angels of God can do but little more than hold in check the host of Satan, that they should not destroy, until further light be given to those in peril, to move them to arouse and look to heaven for help. Jesus will not commission holy angels to extricate those who make no effort to help themselves. If Satan sees he is in danger of losing one soul, he will exert himself to the utmost to keep that one. And when the individual is aroused to his danger, and, with distress and fervor, looks to Jesus for strength, Satan fears he shall lose a captive, and he calls a re-enforcement of his angels to hedge in the poor soul, and form a wall of darkness around him, that heaven's light may not reach him. But if the one in danger perseveres, and in helplessness and weakness casts himself upon the merits of the blood of Christ, Jesus listens to the earnest prayer of faith, and sends a re-enforcement of those angels which excel in strength to deliver him. Satan cannot endure to have his powerful rival appealed to, for he fears and trembles before His [Christ's] strength and majesty. At the sound of fervent prayer, Satan's whole host trembles.... And when angels, all-powerful, clothed with the armory of heaven, come to the help of the fainting, pursued soul, Satan and his host fall back, well knowing that their battle is lost. (*Messages to Young People*, pp. 52, 53)

Every angel would be commissioned to come to our rescue when we thus depend upon Christ rather than that we should be permitted to be overcome. (*That I May Know Him*, p. 265)

Those who realize their weakness trust in a power higher than self. And while they look to God, Satan has no power against them. ("The Danger of Self-Sufficiency," Manuscript 115, 1902)

Praise the Lord even when you fall into darkness. Praise Him even in temptation. 'Rejoice in the Lord alway,' says the apostle; 'and again I say, Rejoice.' (*Testimonies for the Church*, vol. 2, p. 593)

In the darkest days, when appearances seem so forbidding, fear not. Have faith in God. He is working out His will, doing all things well in behalf of His people. The strength of those who love and serve Him will be renewed day by day. His understanding will be placed at their service, that they may not err in the carrying out of His purposes. There is to be no despondency in God's service. Our faith is to endure the pressure brought to bear upon it. God is able and willing to bestow upon His servants all the strength they need. He will more than fulfill the highest expectations of those who put their trust in Him. (*Sons and Daughters of God*, p. 219)

Search for the precious promises of God. If Satan thrusts threatenings before your mind, turn from them and cling to the promises, and let your soul be comforted by their brightness. (*That I May Know Him*, p. 240)

Remember that when God permits the Abyss to be opened, smoke comes from it like the smoke from a gigantic furnace, and the sun and the sky are darkened by the smoke (see Rev. 9:2). Satan is the prince of darkness, and his very presence causes the atmosphere around us to seem dark. Please be aware that this sense of darkness is going to happen much more now that the Holy Spirit is being withdrawn from the earth. Demons will be given more access to people around the world who are not protected by Jesus and His angels. God's people must keep their eyes on Jesus, the Sun of righteousness, as darkness settles upon the earth. Satan will try to discourage you! He will bring up your sins before you; he will send people to aggravate, annoy and distract you; in fact, he will do anything to draw you out of your peace with God and cover you with a mantle of darkness. But you can win the battle by fixing your mind upon the promises of God and placing your faith upon Him!

When trials arise that seem unexplainable, we should not allow our peace to be spoiled. However unjustly we may be treated, let not passion arise. By indulging a spirit of retaliation we injure ourselves. We destroy our own confidence in God, and grieve the Holy Spirit. There is by our side a witness, a heavenly messenger, who will lift up for us a standard against the enemy. *He will shut us in with the bright beams of the Sun of Righteousness. Beyond this Satan cannot penetrate. He cannot pass this shield of holy light. (Christ's Object Lessons, pp. 171, 172, emphasis added)*

For additional help, I have included in the appendix two excellent articles by my friend and co-worker, Christa Negley. May God bless you all as we enter the final battle between the forces of darkness and the forces of light. Keep your eyes on Jesus, and you cannot fail!

How to Cooperate with Jesus in the Final Atonement and Be Sealed

Step 1 - Make a list of all the people in your life for whom you still hold grudges, resentments, complaints or criticisms. This list may include your spouse, children, parents, siblings, extended family members, friends, acquaintances, and work colleagues or anyone who doesn't come up to your expectations or annoys you.

Step 2 - Remember that Christ's blood has already paid for their sins and that He alone has the right to judge them.

Step 3 - When no one else comes to your mind, ask God if there is anyone else that you may have forgotten to list. God will bring that person to consciousness.

Step 4 - Take each person and make a list of all the hurts and wrongs that you feel have been committed against you. Even if they have denied doing you wrong, remember that it is your perception and reality that needs to be dealt with.

Step 5 - Give each incident specifically to Jesus and tell Him that you do not want to carry it or remember it anymore. Love "keeps no record of wrongs" (1 Cor. 13:5).

Step 6 - Ask Jesus to forgive you for your resentments, complaints, and criticisms that you have harbored in your heart in response to the injustices done to you. Ask Him to forgive you for your wrong reactions. Then ask Jesus to give you His forgiveness for each person that has injured you—you do not have to generate this forgiveness.

Step 7 - Ask Jesus to cleanse your mind of all the negative emotions, hurts, and pain that have been stored there as a result of the injury or abuse.

Step 8 - Ask Jesus to remove all the demons involved with these sins and to send the demons to the abyss and only to the abyss.

Step 9 - Ask Jesus to cleanse your books in Heaven.

Step 10 - Ask Him to give you His thoughts about all these individuals. Ask Him to give you His love for everyone and to fill you with the Holy Spirit.

Step 11 - Ask Jesus to seal you on all these points that you have confessed so that you will never again take up these offenses. Claim Isaiah 26:12–14, the blotting out of sin:

> Lord, you establish peace for us; all that we have accomplished you have done for us. Lord our God, other lords besides you have ruled over us, but your name alone do we honor. They are now dead, they live no more; their spirits do not rise. You punished them and brought them to ruin; you wiped out all memory of them.

Step 12 - Claim Colossians 3:3: "For you died, and your life is now hidden with Christ in God." Pray to be filled with the latter rain and be prepared to give the loud cry. Ask God to give you a love for souls and to see each person you meet through His eyes.

Step 13 - Claim the promise found in Matthew 15:13. "He replied, 'Every plant that my heavenly Father has not planted will be pulled up by the roots.'"

> The plant of love must be carefully nourished, else it will die. Every good principle must be cherished if we would have it thrive in the soul. That which Satan plants in the heart,—envy, jealousy, evil surmising, evil speaking, impatience, prejudice, selfishness, covetousness, and vanity,—must be uprooted. If these evil things are allowed to remain in the soul, they will bear fruit by which many shall be defiled. ("The Sacred Duties of Home Life," *The Signs of the Times*, 1892)

These steps can be applied to any sin that you may be struggling with, any negative emotion that plagues you such as fear, anxiety, depression, etc., and any demon that harasses or oppresses you. The sins and negative emotions then become an open door for Satan to tempt or harass you.

Compare your feelings with the fruit of the Spirit as listed in Galatians 5:22–24. Anything negative is not inspired by the Holy Spirit. The roots of evil that Satan has sown in our hearts must be uprooted. Dwelling on negative things can cause us to connect with another spirit. In Hebrews 12:14–16, we read, "Make every effort to live in peace with everyone and to be holy; without holiness no one will see the Lord. See to it that no one falls short of the grace of God and that no bitter root grows up to cause trouble and defile many."

Written by Christa Negley, MCC

Walking in the Light of God's Presence

Have you ever wondered why one moment you seem to feel so happy and joyous and then suddenly everything is changed, and you find yourself feeling discouraged, depressed, disheartened, and negative? God seems so far away, and the future looks forbidding. You cannot penetrate the darkness, and it hangs over you like a cloud.

There are many reasons why we fall into the darkness and our minds connect with the mind of the enemy. At any given moment our minds are either under the power of the Holy Spirit or the power of the evil one. There is no third option.

> Unless we do yield ourselves to the control of Christ, we shall be dominated by the wicked one. We must inevitably be under the control of the one or the other of the two great powers that are contending for the supremacy of the world. It is not necessary for us deliberately to choose the service of the kingdom of darkness in order to come under its dominion. We have only to neglect to ally ourselves with the kingdom of light. If we do not co-operate with the heavenly agencies, Satan will take possession of the heart, and will make it his abiding place. The only defense against evil is the indwelling of Christ in the heart through faith in His righteousness. (*The Desire of Ages*, 324)

When we are under the Spirit of God, then the fruit of the Spirit will be evident in our lives, including love, joy, peace, long-suffering, kindness, goodness, meekness, gentleness, and self-control. God is now trying to bring His people to the point where they will not respond to the voice of the enemy and follow his biddings. John 10:5 tells us that His sheep do not listen to the voice of the stranger. This is all part of the process of the judgment where God shows us those things in our lives that still connect us with the thoughts and feelings (character) of the evil one and enslave us to His negativity.

Although this is not intended to be an exhaustive list, here are some of the common causes that bring our minds into darkness: fears of any kind, including anxiety or worry of what may happen in the future, fears about the time of trouble, fears of the economic collapse, fears that we won't gain the victory, fears about the salvation of our loves ones, fears that we will lose our job, fears about the closing of probation, fears that all our sins aren't forgiven, fears of being criticized, fears that we will not receive the latter rain, fears of getting old and dying, fears of personal rejection, fears that we aren't going to make it, fears of our own value and worth, fears that we won't fulfill God's blueprint for our lives, the ramifications of the Sunday law, and so forth.

Looking at our own defects or the faults of others can bring us into darkness, as does comparing ourselves with others. We can fall into darkness after being drawn into an argument with someone, becoming angry, frustrated, blaming others, wallowing in our own guilt, or anything that puts us into a negative frame of mind. We can also become overwhelmed when we look at the amount of work that still needs to be done in the world and carry burdens that Jesus has promised to carry for us and for His church.

We sometimes take on responsibilities that the Lord has not laid upon us and thus fall into darkness because the load it too heavy for us, and He is not helping us carry it. We must remember that He is there to help us accomplish all that He bids us do. We are not promised grace for tomorrow, and living with today's grace will not suffice for the problems of tomorrow. If our minds are not connecting with praise, we are not in the sanctuary, but we are somewhere else.

All our tomorrows are in the hands of the Omnipotent God, not in the feeble hands of humanity. That is why we are told not to be anxious about tomorrow. No wonder the Scriptures tell us in the time of the end that men's hearts will fail them as they look at the things that are coming on the earth (see Luke 21:26, KJV). Satan loves to get our eyes off of Jesus and have us focus on our problems instead of bringing our problems, our fears, and our sins to Him.

It was one morning a couple of weeks ago that I found myself in a state of darkness. I had been struggling with a particular issue time and time again and could not resolve it in my mind. I didn't even think that God had the answers, although intellectually I knew different. I prayed and pleaded with

God to help me get out of the pit I had fallen into. He answered my prayer by teaching me a new principle that I had never focused on before. It changed my life, and it is my prayer that it will change yours too.

He brought to my mind a phrase found in 1 John 1:5. It reads: "God is light; in him there is no darkness at all." Note carefully—no darkness at all. Obviously, if I was in the darkness and since He is in the light, then I must not be where He is. My reality was not God's reality. So in order to come into the light and stay in the light, I needed to be with Him and focus on His reality. The passage continues by saying, "But if we walk in the light, as he is in the light, we have fellowship one with another" (verse 7).

We do not possess the answers to our problems; many times we are not capable of resolving issues that come up, difficulties that confront us, or accusing tongues that malign us. But God does. His reality is all light because He already knows how He is going to get us through the darkness of our reality. He already has the solution to our every problem. He has the resources needed and all the wisdom of the eternal ages at His disposal. He has millions of angels to execute His commands in our behalf if needed.

So I claimed this text and asked God to connect me with His reality, and in exchange, I chose to give Him my perspective. By faith, we can always stay in that light because the government of our lives, our church, and of our country is in His hands. All I needed to do was to give it to Him and trust Him to see me through. He will even teach us to be very sensitive to our own spirits and warn us whenever we are tempted to look at the darkness that threatens to engulf us.

"We do not look at the things which are seen, but at the things which are not seen" (2 Cor. 4:18, NKJV). When Jesus was in the boat on the Sea of Galilee, He certainly wasn't focusing on the waves. He was so connected with the Light of heaven that He could rest His life in the arms of His Father. He wasn't worried and anxious or losing sleep over it. But what were disciples looking at? The wind and the waves. And so they battled on until they recognized that their resources were failing and to all appearances it looked like they were about to drown. Imagine that, Jesus was with them, and they really thought they were going to drown.

I want to share with you some of the beautiful quotations and Scriptures that are so apropos to this subject.

> Take courage in the Lord. Close the windows of the soul earthward, and open them heavenward. If your voices are uplifted in prayer to heaven for light, the Lord Jesus, who is light and life, peace and joy, will hear your cry. He, the Sun of Righteousness, will shine into the chambers of your mind, lighting up the soul tem-

ple…. Welcome the sunshine of His presence into your home. (*The Adventist Home*, p. 343)

In Christ is light and peace and joy forevermore. (The Adventist Home, p. 431)

If I should look at the dark clouds—the troubles and perplexities that come to me in my work—I should have time to do nothing else. But I know that there is light and glory beyond the clouds. By faith I reach through the darkness to the glory. (*Mind, Character, and Personality*, vol. 2, p. 493)

Jesus is attractive. He is full of love, mercy, and compassion. He proposes to be our friend, to walk with us through all the rough pathways of life. He says to us, I am the Lord thy God; walk with Me, and I will fill thy path with light. Jesus, the Majesty of Heaven, proposes to elevate to companionship with himself those who come to Him with their burdens, their weaknesses, and their cares. ("Rest in Christ," *The Signs of the Times*, 1887)

The Lord is my light and my salvation—whom shall I fear? (Ps. 27:1)

You need not be surprised if everything in the journey heavenward is not pleasant. There is no use in looking to our own defects. Looking unto Jesus, the darkness passes away, and the true light shineth…. All the paths of life are beset with peril, but we are safe if we follow where the Master leads the way, trusting the One whose voice we hear saying, 'Follow Me.' 'He that followeth Me shall not walk in darkness, but shall have the light of life.' (*The Seventh-day Adventist Bible Commentary*, vol. 3, p. 1143)

God has already rescued us from the kingdom of darkness and now He wants us to walk in the light of His presence. It was on Calvary that He battled the darkness for us so we no longer have to remain within its grasp. Not only did He gain the victory over our sins but He also carried our every negative emotion and infirmity. We can live in His love and be filled with His peace. What a wonderful God!

But you are a chosen people, a royal priesthood, a holy nation, God's special possession, that you may declare the praises of him who called you out of darkness into his wonderful light. (1 Peter 2:9)

For he has rescued us from the dominion of darkness and brought us into the kingdom of the Son he loves. (Col. 1:13)

I will lead the blind by ways they have not known, along unfamiliar paths I will guide them; I will turn the darkness into light before them and make the rough places smooth. These are the things I will do; I will not forsake them. (Isa. 42:16)

But even if we should fall into the darkness, God has promised to bring us out into the light of His presence again. Look carefully at the following texts:

The LORD turns my darkness into light. (2 Sam. 22:29)

He brought them out of darkness, the utter darkness, and broke away their chains. (Ps. 107:14)

Suppose we make a mistake, maybe even commit sin in thought or in word. It is then that Satan delights to have us wallow in guilt and self-recrimination. We must remember that God sees our weaknesses and has compassion on us. Our faith must connect with the truth that our sins have already been forgiven, and His grace has been graciously extended to us. We can claim that forgiveness and bask in the light of His presence. Satan has already been defeated, and the power of darkness over us is broken.

Praise the Lord even when you fall into darkness. Praise Him even in temptation. 'Rejoice in the Lord alway,' says the apostle; 'and again I say, Rejoice....' You will thus gather rays of eternal light from the throne of glory and scatter them around you. (*Testimonies for the Church*, vol. 2, pp. 593, 594)

When the enemy seeks to enshroud the soul with darkness, sing faith and talk faith, and you will find that you have sung and talked yourself into the light. (Counsels to Parents, Teachers, and Students, p. 234)

In conclusion, I would like to quote some paragraphs from the book *Early Writings*. What is stated here can be applied anytime we find ourselves in darkness. This process is a battle, but with Jesus victory is guaranteed.

I saw some, with strong faith and agonizing cries, pleading with God. Their countenances were pale and marked with deep anxiety, expressive of their internal struggle. Firmness and great earnestness was expressed in their countenances; large drops of perspiration fell from their foreheads. Now and then their faces would light up with the marks of God's approbation, and again the same solemn, earnest, anxious look would settle upon them. Evil angels crowded around, pressing darkness upon them to shut out Jesus from their view, that their eyes might be drawn to the darkness that surrounded them, and thus they be led to distrust God and murmur against Him. Their only safety was in keeping their eyes directed upward. Angels of God had charge over His people, and as the poisonous atmosphere of evil angels was pressed around these anxious ones, the heavenly angels were continually wafting their wings over them to scatter the thick darkness. As the praying ones continued their earnest cries, at times a ray of light from Jesus came to them, to encourage their hearts and light up their countenances. Some, I saw, did not participate in this work of agonizing and pleading. They seemed indifferent and careless. They were not resisting the darkness around them, and it shut them in like a thick cloud. The angels of God left these and went to the aid of the earnest, praying ones. I saw angels of God hasten to the assistance of all who were struggling with all their power to resist the evil angels and trying to help themselves by calling upon God with perseverance. (pp. 269, 270)

It is a struggle to resist the darkness that the demons bring into our lives, but Jesus has promised to send us help from the sanctuary. As we commune with Him, He will bring us out of the darkness and keep us connected with Him. He will keep us safe in His presence where all is light, joy, and peace.

It is impossible to give any idea of the experience of the people of God who shall be alive upon the earth when celestial glory and a repetition of the persecutions of the past are blended. They will walk in the light proceeding from the throne of God. By means of the angels there will be constant communication between heaven and earth. (*Testimonies for the Church*, vol. 9, p. 16)

There is not an impulse of our nature, not a faculty of the mind or an inclination of the heart, but needs to be, moment by moment, under the control of the Spirit of God. There is not a blessing which God bestows upon man, nor a trial which he permits to befall him, but Satan both can and will seize upon it to tempt, to harass, and destroy the soul, if we give him the least advantage. Therefore however great one's spiritual light, however much he may enjoy of the divine favor and blessing, he should ever walk humbly before the Lord, pleading in faith that God will direct every thought and control every impulse. (*Messages to Young People*, p. 62)

Soon and very soon the floodgates of heaven will open wide, and God will pour the latter rain upon His people who have been preparing themselves by walking in all the light that He has already been sending them. They have treasured the light and have cooperated with Him in rejecting all the darkness of the enemy. They will then be privileged to receive all the light needed to proclaim earth's final message.

> Arise, shine; for thy light is come, and the glory of the LORD is risen upon thee. For, behold, the darkness shall cover the earth, and gross darkness the people: but the LORD shall arise upon thee, and his glory shall be seen upon thee. And the Gentiles shall come to thy light, and kings to the brightness of thy rising. (Isa. 60:1–3, KJV)

It is my prayer that each of you will so connect with the light of heaven that even the darkness of this world will be as light to you because everything will be seen from God's perspective and not your own. "Even the darkness will not be dark to you; the night will shine like the day, for darkness is as light to you" (Ps. 139:12). May God's blessing rest upon you as you bask in the sunshine of His love and live in the safety of His presence.

Written and compiled by Christa Negley, MCC

Bibliography

Ellen G. White, "Rest in Christ," *The Signs of the Times*, 1887.

Ellen G. White, "The Sacred Duties of Home Life," *The Sign of the Times*, 1892.

White, Ellen G. *The Adventist Home*. Hagerstown, MD: Review and Herald Publishing Association, 1952.

White, Ellen G. *Christ's Object Lessons*. Washington, DC: Review and Herald Publishing Association, 1900.

White, Ellen G. *Counsels to Parents, Teachers, and Students*. Mountain View, CA: Pacific Press Publishing Association, 1913.

White, Ellen G. *The Desire of Ages*. Mountain View, CA: Pacific Press Publishing Association, 1898.

White, Ellen G. *Early Writings*. Washington, DC: Review and Herald Publishing Association, 1882.

White, Ellen G. *From Trials to Triumph*. Mountain View, CA: Pacific Press Publishing Association, 1984.

White, Ellen G. *The Great Controversy*. Mountain View, CA: Pacific Press Publishing Association, 1911.

White, Ellen G. *The Great Controversy 1888*. Mountain View, CA: Pacific Press Publishing Association, 1888.

White, Ellen G. *In Heavenly Places*. Washington, DC: Review and Herald Publishing Association, 1967.

White, Ellen G. *Last Day Events*. Boise, ID: Pacific Press Publishing Association, 1992.

White, Ellen. G. *Lt-233,* 1904. Ellen Gould White, 1904.

White, Ellen G. *Maranatha*. Washington, DC: Review and Herald Publishing Association, 1976.

White, Ellen G. *Medical Ministry*. Mountain View, CA: Pacific Press Publishing Association, 1932.

White, Ellen G. *Messages to Young People*. Hagerstown, MD: Review and Herald Publishing Association, 1930.

White, Ellen G. *Mind, Character, and Personality*. Vol. 2. Nashville, TN: Southern Publishing Association, 1977.

White, Ellen G. *The Ministry of Healing*. Mountain View, CA: Pacific Press Publishing Association, 1905.

White, Ellen. G. *Ms 115, 1902*. Ellen Gould White, 1902.

White, Ellen G. *My Life Today*. Washington, DC: Review and Herald Publishing Association, 1952.

White, Ellen G. *Our High Calling*. Washington, DC: Review and Herald Publishing Association, 1961.

Bibliography

White, Ellen G. *Patriarchs and Prophets*. Washington, DC: Review and Herald Publishing Association, 1890.

White, Ellen G. *Reflecting Christ.* Hagerstown, MD: Review and Herald Publishing Association, 1985.

White, Ellen G. The SDA Bible Commentary. Vol. 1. Washington, DC: Review and Herald Publishing Association, 1953.

White, Ellen G. The SDA Bible Commentary. Vol. 3. Washington, DC: Review and Herald Publishing Association, 1954.

White, Ellen G. *The SDA Bible Commentary*. Vol. 4. Washington, DC: Review and Herald Publishing Association, 1955.

White, Ellen G. *The SDA Bible Commentary*. Vol. 5. Washington, DC: Review and Herald Publishing Association, 1956.

White, Ellen G. *The SDA Bible Commentary*. Vol. 6. Washington, DC: Review and Herald Publishing Association, 1956.

White, Ellen G. *The SDA Bible Commentary*. Vol. 7. Washington, DC: Review and Herald Publishing Association, 1957.

White, Ellen G. *The SDA Bible Commentary*. Vol. 8. Washington, DC: Review and Herald Publishing Association, 1960.

White, Ellen G. *Selected Messages*. Book 2. Washington, DC: Review and Herald Publishing Association, 1958.

White, Ellen G. *Selected Messages*. Book 3. Washington, DC: Review and Herald Publishing Association, 1980.

White, Ellen G. *Sons and Daughters of God*. Washington, DC: Review and Herald Publishing Association, 1955.

White, Ellen G. *Testimonies for the Church*. Vol. 1. Mountain View, CA: Pacific Press Publishing Association, 1868.

White, Ellen G. *Testimonies for the Church*. Vol. 2. Mountain View, CA: Pacific Press Publishing Association, 1871.

White, Ellen G. *Testimonies for the Church*. Vol. 4. Mountain View, CA: Pacific Press Publishing Association, 1881.

White, Ellen G. *Testimonies for the Church*. Vol. 5. Mountain View, CA: Pacific Press Publishing Association, 1889.

White, Ellen G. *Testimonies for the Church*. Vol. 6. Mountain View, CA: Pacific Press Publishing Association, 1901.

White, Ellen G. *Testimonies for the Church*. Vol. 8. Mountain View, CA: Pacific Press Publishing Association, 1904.

White, Ellen G. *Testimonies for the Church*. Vol. 9. Mountain View, CA: Pacific Press Publishing Association, 1909.

White, Ellen G. *That I May Know Him*. Washington, DC: Review and Herald Publishing Association, 1964.

White, Ellen G. *This Day With God.* Washington, DC: Review and Herald Publishing Association, 1979.

White, Ellen G. *Thoughts from the Mount of Blessing*. Mountain View, CA: Pacific Press Publishing Association, 1896.

White, Ellen G. *The Upward Look*. Washington, DC: Review and Herald Publishing Association, 1982.

We invite you to view the complete
selection of titles we publish at:

www.TEACHServices.com

Scan with your mobile
device to go directly
to our website.

Please write or email us your praises, reactions, or
thoughts about this or any other book we publish at:

www.TEACHServices.com • (800) 367-1844

P.O. Box 954
Ringgold, GA 30736

info@TEACHServices.com

TEACH Services, Inc., titles may be purchased in bulk for
educational, business, fund-raising, or sales promotional use.
For information, please e-mail:

BulkSales@TEACHServices.com

Finally, if you are interested in seeing
your own book in print, please contact us at

publishing@TEACHServices.com

We would be happy to review your manuscript for free.